DUOLOGUES
FOR BOYS & GIRLS
from ages 8-14yrs

Copyright © 2020 Kim Gilbert
All rights reserved
ISBN: 9798579607577

DEDICATION

This collection of acting duologues is dedicated to all teachers and students of drama with a love of performing from the classics. There is something for every young performer to choose from. All of the characters in this book have been chosen carefully and are most suited to the 8-14 yr age range. These scenes are suitable for a wide range of study, performance, exams and festivals.

ACKNOWLEDGEMENTS

A special thanks goes to my husband Steve, who has prepared this collection for publication, and has bailed me out on numerous occasions over the years, with his technical expertise.

TABLE OF CONTENTS

Introduction	1
Acting a role	2
Acting Style	4

Boy/Boy Duologues

Pinocchio

Gepetto & Pinocchio	7
Cricket & Pinocchio	10

Tom Sawyer

Tom and a Boy	15
Tom & Ben	18

Puss in Boots

Puss & The Miller	21

Toad of Toad Hall

Rat & Mole 1	27
Rat & Mole 2	31
Rat & Mole 3	36

Lord Arthur Savile's Crime:

Lord Arthur & Herr Winckelkopf 1	40
Lord Arthur & Herr Winckelkopf 2	43

The Importance of Being Earnest:

Jack & Algernon 1	47
Jack & Algernon 2	52

Jack & Algernon 3	56
<u>Winnie-the-Pooh:</u>	
Rabbit & Pooh	61
## <u>Boy/Girl Duologues</u>	**64**
<u>Winnie-the-Pooh:</u>	
Kanga & Pooh	65
Kanga & Roo	69
<u>The Ugly Duckling</u>	
Prince & Princess	74
<u>Peter Pan</u>	
Peter Pan & Wendy	82
<u>Rumplestilkskin</u>	
Rumplestiltskin & the Miller's Daughter	88
<u>Toad of Toad Hall</u>	
Toad & Phoebe	90
<u>The Magician's Nephew</u>	
Digory & Polly	94
<u>A Little Princess</u>	
Sara & Papa	98
<u>Pinocchio</u>	
Pinocchio & the Fairy 1	101
Pinocchio & the Fairy 2	105

The Snow Queen

Gerda & Karl — 109

Gerda & Kay — 112

Tom Sawyer

Becky & Tom — 115

Little Women

Jo & Laurie 1 — 119

Jo & Laurie 2 — 124

Rebecca of Sunnybrook Farm

Rebecca & Aladdin — 129

Back to Methuselah

Eve & Serpent — 134

Pygmalion

Eliza & Prof Higgins 1 — 138

Eliza & Prof Higgins 2 — 144

Girl/Girl Duologues — 146

Little Women

Jo & Amy — 147

Jo & Meg — 152

The Secret Garden

Mary & Martha — 155

The Princess & The Players

Elizabeth & Anne — 160

Beauty & the Beast

Jessamine & Jonquiline   164

The Wizard of Oz

Dorothy & the Good Witch   169

Anne of Green Gables

Anne & Marilla   173

Anne & Diana   176

A Little Princess

Sara & Ermengarde 1   179

Sara & Becky   183

Sara & Miss Minchin   187

Sara & Ermengarde 2   191

I Capture the Castle

Rose & Cassandra   194

INTRODUCTION

I have compiled and edited this collection of Classic duologues for young boys and girls to study, perform and enjoy. These scenes are suitable for a range of acting exams and awards as well as for auditions and festivals. I have tried and tested these scenes with numerous students over the years with great success and more importantly, they have thoroughly enjoyed working on them. It is important to choose characters within ones' playing range. This collection contains a range of characters suited to be played by young boys and girls from the age of approximately 8yrs to 14 yrs. From my experience, I have seen many young actors tackling characters which are often unsuited to their age range and skills.

There will be plenty of time in the future to tackle the more mature and demanding male characters which are available to play from a wealth of drama and literature. Learn to build your skills and technique slowly and systematically with the younger, and age-appropriate characters before you attempt to move forwards to the demands of older and more complex characters.

The duologues in this collection are taken from a range of plays and classic novels: Peter Pan, The Secret Garden, The Wizard of Oz, Tom Sawyer, The Wind in the Willows, Winnie the Pooh, Pinocchio, Beauty & the Beast, Little Women, Rebecca of Sunnybrook Farm and many more. Each scene has an introduction prepared suitable for exam or festival work and are also timed with exams and festival work in mind. I hope you enjoy this collection.

ACTING A ROLE

When preparing for acting a role one should always study the play as a whole if you can and approach your chosen scene in context within the whole play.

Here are some questions to consider:

Is your character a central character or a leading character?

Is your character crucial to the development of the plot?

Perhaps your character is a stock character or small cameo role, providing a sub-plot, comedy or light relief to the plot?

Consider what your character looks like in terms of physical appearance? This can be considered in terms of age, height, physique, posture, colouring etc.

How do you envisage your character in costume? Do you need to consider the historical period for your chosen role and research the type of costume you would be wearing?

Think about how you might like to play your character in terms of physical and vocal skills? Is your natural voice appropriate or do you need to characterise your voice and speak with an accent or dialect?

How does your character develop throughout the play? Try to map your character's journey throughout the play?

What are your character's likes, dislikes?

How do you relate to your character and how does your character relate to the other characters in the play?

What do you like about your character? Try to create a backstory for your character.

What is your character's role/purpose in the play? Try to establish his/her objective within the scene you are playing or even in the play as a whole.

Consider casting. Is this role a good choice for you? Does this character suit your acting skills and personality?

What skills and characteristics do you need as an actor to play this character?

ACTING STYLE

It is important to adopt the correct style of acting for your chosen performance piece. You will need to consider whether your scene is perhaps from the realist school of writing, or whether you are performing Shakespeare and need to acquire knowledge of the metre which Shakespeare writes in. Or perhaps you have chosen a piece which relies purely on fantasy and imagination. These are all choices you will have to consider when tackling a scene.

Fantasy

This style of acting has no limitations. In fantasy, anything can happen in fantasy stories and the actor has great scope to use their imagination. This style is not to be taken too seriously and offers the young actor great creativity. Many children's plays involve fantasy and are popular choices with young players. These plays are a good starting point for young actors. The style of acting is often larger than life and 'overacting' in these types of roles is common and acceptable.

Comedy and Tragedy

It is necessary to identify the genre of your play as this will affect your playing style. Good timing is essential in comedy and many roles will require a heightened use of realism to create the desired comic effect. However, if you are playing tragedy, a more serious and sombre acting style will be required. There are many styles of acting and these need to be identified and an appropriate playing style adopted, according to the writing style of your chosen play.

Realism

Realism, is a literary technique which describes locations, characters and themes in a realistic style without using elaborate imagery or rhetorical language. This means that the emotions of the characters have to be sincere and believable.

Playing the Objective

The Theatre Practitioner, Constantine Stanislavski, suggested that a whole play be separated into a series of smaller scenes or units of performance. In each unit there will be an objective. The objectives from these units will form or lead to a Super objective.

Basically, playing the objective means identifying what your character is trying to achieve in each scene? What is your character's motivation? If this goal can be established, the performer will have discovered an overall objective.

When analyzing a play, you should look for its' overall aim or theme. The scenes can be broken up into parts. Decide on the objective for each scene or unit. Ideally, the objective should be considered as a verb, an action; something your character ideally wants to do or achieve

The Super-Objective

It helps to work out what the super-objective of the play is, as a whole. It must be the fundamental driving force of the whole play. The super objective is easy to determine in a well-written play. The objective should be described in terms of a verb. The "through line of action" must guide everything towards the super objective.

Period

You should be aware of the period of the writing style and consider the manners which were used during this time. This also means considering the costumes worn during the period.

Truth

The actor should always aim to perform with truth, imagination and sincerity. Spontaneity in acting and is key in order to convince your audience of your credibility.

BOY/BOY DUOLOGUES

PINOCCHIO
BY CARLO COLLODI (1883)

(Pinocchio returns home from his travels as he is hungry. Geppetto, Pinocchio's father, gives Pinocchio his own breakfast).

Geppetto:
Open the door!

Pinocchio:
Dear papa, I cannot!

Geppetto:
Why can't you?

Pinocchio:
Because my feet have been eaten.

Geppetto:
And who has eaten your feet?

Pinocchio:
The cat.

Geppetto:
Open the door, I tell you! If you don't, when I get into the house you shall have the cat from me!

Pinocchio:
I cannot stand up, believe me. Oh, poor me! Poor me! I shall have to walk on my knees for the rest of my life!

(Geppetto takes pity on Pinocchio).

Geppetto:
My little Pinocchio! How did you manage to burn your feet?

Pinocchio:
I don't know, papa, but it has been such a dreadful night that I shall remember it as long as I live. It thundered and lightened, and I was very hungry, and then the Talking-Cricket said to me: 'It serves you right; you have been wicked and you deserve it' and I said to him: 'Take care, Cricket! and he said: 'You are a puppet and you have a wooden head,' and I threw the handle of
a hammer at him, and he died, but the fault was his, for I didn't wish to kill him. And I returned home at once, and because I was always hungry. I put my feet on the brazier to dry them, and then you returned, and I found they were burnt off, and I am always hungry, but I have no longer any feet! Oh! Oh! Oh! Oh! (*He cries*).

Geppetto:
These three pears were intended for my breakfast, but I will give them to you willingly. Eat them, and I hope they will do you good.

Pinocchio:
If you wish me to eat them, be kind enough to peel them for me.

Geppetto:
Peel them? I should never have thought, my boy, that you were so dainty and fastidious. That is bad! In this world we should accustom ourselves from childhood to like and to eat everything, for there is no saying to what we may be brought. There are so many chances!

Pinocchio:
You are no doubt right, but I will never eat fruit that has not been peeled. I cannot bear rind.

(Geppetto peels the fruit for Pinocchio. When Pinocchio eats the fruit, he starts to throw away the core).

Geppetto:
Do not throw it away; in this world everything may be of use.

Pinocchio:
But core I am determined I will not eat. I am as hungry as ever!

Geppetto:
But, my boy, I have nothing more to give you! I have only the rind and the cores of the three pears.

Pinocchio:
I must have patience! If there is nothing else, I will eat a rind.
(He suddenly realises the core and the rind does not taste so bad). Ah! Now I feel comfortable.

Geppetto:
You see, now, that I was right when I said to you that it did not do to accustom ourselves to be too particular or too dainty in our tastes. We can never know, my dear boy, what may happen to us. There are so many chances!

PINOCCHIO
BY CARLO COLLODI

(On his travels, Pinocchio meets a talking cricket named Jiminy Cricket).

<u>Cricket:</u>
Cri-cri-cri…

<u>Pinocchio:</u>
Who calls me? *(He is frightened).*

<u>Cricket:</u>
It is I!

<u>Pinocchio:</u>
Tell me, Cricket, who may you be?

<u>Cricket:</u>
I am the Talking-Cricket, and I have lived in this room a hundred years or more.

<u>Pinocchio:</u>
Now, however, this room is mine, and if you would do me a pleasure go away at once, without even turning round.

<u>Cricket:</u>
I will not go until I have told you a great truth.

<u>Pinocchio:</u>
Tell it me, then, and be quick about it.

<u>Cricket:</u>
Woe to those boys who rebel against their parents and run

away from home. They will never come to any good in the world, and sooner or later they will repent bitterly.

Pinocchio:
Sing away, Cricket, as you please, and as long as you please. For me, I have made up my mind to run away tomorrow at daybreak, because if I remain, I shall not escape the fate of all other boys; I shall be sent to school and shall be made to study either by love or by force. To tell you in confidence, I have no wish to learn; it is much more amusing to run after butterflies, or to climb trees and to take the young birds out of their nests.

Cricket:
Poor little goose! But do you not know that in that way you will grow up a perfect donkey, and that everyone will make fun of you?

Pinocchio:
Hold your tongue, you wicked, ill-omened croaker!

Cricket:
But if you do not wish to go to school why not at least learn a trade, if only to enable you to earn honestly a piece of bread!

Pinocchio:
Do you want me to tell you? Amongst all the trades in the world there is only one that really takes my fancy.

Cricket:
And that trade – what is it?

Pinocchio:
It is to eat, drink, sleep and amuse myself, and to lead a vagabond life from morning to night.

Cricket:
As a rule, all those who follow that trade, end almost always either in a hospital or in a prison.

Pinocchio:
Take care, you wicked, ill-omened croaker! Woe to you if I fly into
a passion!

Cricket:
Poor Pinocchio! I really pity you!

Pinocchio:
Why do you pity me?

Cricket:
Because you are a puppet and, what is worse, because you have a wooden head.

(Pinocchio jumps up in a rage and snatches a wooden hammer and throws it at the Talking-Cricket. The hammer strikes the cricket on the head and the Cricket is flattened against the wall).

Cricket:
Cri-cri –cri-! *(He dies).*

Pinocchio:
The Talking-Cricket was right. I did wrong to rebel against my papa and to run away from home. If my papa were

here, I should not now be dying of yawning! Oh, what a dreadful illness hunger is!

TOM SAWYER
BY MARK TWAIN

(Tom meets a boy a bit larger than himself. The boy is a newcomer to the village of St. Petersburg. The boy is well dressed and is wearing a cap and blue cloth suit. He wears a necktie with a bright bit of ribbon. He looked 'citified'. He behaves in a snobby fashion and makes Tom feel shabby. When one boy moves, the other moves – but only sideways, in a circle; they keep face to face and eye to eye all the time).

<u>Tom:</u>
I can lick you!

<u>Boy:</u>
I'd like to see you try it.

<u>Tom:</u>
Well, I can do it.

<u>Boy:</u>
No, you can't, either.

<u>Tom:</u>
Yes, I can.

<u>Boy:</u>
No, you can't.

<u>Tom:</u>
I can.

Boy:
You can't.

Tom:
Can.

Boy:
Can't.

Tom:
What's your name?

Boy:
T'isn't any of your business, maybe.

Tom:
Well, I vow I'll make it my business.

Boy:
Well, why don't you?

Tom:
If you say much, I will.

Boy:
Much – much – MUCH. There now!

Tom:
Oh, you think you're mighty smart, don't you? I could lick you with
one hand tied behind me, if I wanted to.

Boy:
Well, why don't you do it? You say you can do it.

<u>Tom:</u>
Well, I will, if you fool with me.

<u>Boy:</u>
Oh, yes – I've seen whole families in the same fix.

<u>Tom:</u>
Smarty! You think you're something, now, don't you? Oh, what a hat.

<u>Boy:</u>
You can lump that hat if you don't like it. I dare you to knock it off – and anybody that'll take a dare will suck eggs.

<u>Tom:</u>
You're a liar!

<u>Boy:</u>
You're another.

<u>Tom:</u>
You're a fighting liar and doesn't take it up.

<u>Boy:</u>
TAKE A WALK!

<u>Tom:</u>
Say – if you give me much more of your sass, I'll take a bunce and rock it off your head.

<u>Boy:</u>
Oh, of course you will.

<u>Tom:</u>
Well, I will.

Boy:
Well, why don't you do it then? What do you keep saying you
will for? Why don't you *do* it? It's because you're afraid.
Tom:
I aint afraid

Boy:
You are

Tom:
I ain't

Boy:
You are.
(the boys sidle around each other again).

Tom:
Get away from here.

Boy:
Go away yourself!

Tom:
I won't.

Boy:
I won't either.
(They are both shoving with all their might and glowering at each other with hatred, but neither can get an advantage).

Tom:
You're a coward and a pup. I'll tell my big brother on you, and he can thrash you with his little finger, and I'll make him do it, too.

Boy:
What do I care for your big brother? I've got a brother that's bigger than he is – and what's more he can throw him over that fence too.

Tom:
That's a lie.

(They are both lying).

Boy:
Your saying so don't make it so.

Tom:
I dare you to step over that, and I'll lick you till you can't stand up. Anybody that'll take a dare will steal sheep.

Boy:
Now you said you'd do it – why don't you do it?

Tom:
By jingo! For two cents I *will* do it.

(The boy takes two cents out of his pocket and holds them out with derision. Tom strikes them to the ground. The boys fight again. Tom ends up seated astride the boy).

Boy:
Holler 'nuff! *(He is crying)* Holler 'Nuff. Nuff!
(Tom allows him to stand up)

Tom:
Now that'll learn you. Better lookout who you're fooling with next time. *(Tom chases the boy away).*

TOM SAWYER
BY MARK TWAIN

(Tom has the task of painting a fence. His friend, Ben, comes along nibbling an apple. The story is set in America).

Tom:
Why, it's you, Ben! I weren't noticing.

Ben:
Say – I'm going in a swimming, I am. Don't you wish you could? But of course, you'd rather work – wouldn't you? Course you would!

Tom:
What do you call work?

Ben:
Why, ain't that work?

Tom:
Well, maybe it is, and maybe it ain't. All I know, is, it suits Tom Sawyer.

Ben:
Oh come, now, you don't mean to let on that you *like* it?

Tom:
Like it? Well, I don't see why I oughtn't to like it. Does a boy get a chance to whitewash a fence every day?

(Tom continues painting. Ben watches with interest).

Ben:
Say, Tom, let *me* whitewash a little.

Tom:
No – no – I reckon it wouldn't hardly do, Ben. You see, Aunt Polly's awful particular about this fence – right here on the street, you know – but if it was the back fence I wouldn't mind and she wouldn't either. Yes, she's awful particular about this fence; it's got to be done very careful; I reckon there ain't one boy in a thousand, maybe two thousand, that can do it the way it's got to be done.

Ben:
Is that so? Oh come, now – lemme just try. Only just a little – I'd let *you*, if you was me, Tom.

Tom:
I'd like to, honest indian; but Aunt Polly – well, Jim wanted to do it, but she wouldn't let him; Sid wanted to do it, and she wouldn't let Sid. Now don't you see how I'm fixed? If *you* was to tackle this fence and anything was to happen to it –

Ben:
Oh, shucks, I'll be just as careful. Now lemme try. Say – I'll give you the core of my apple.

Tom:
Well, here – No, Ben, now don't. I'm afeard – *(Tom gives Ben the brush with reluctance on his face but joy in his heart. Tom sits and enjoys the apple whilst Ben slaves away painting the fence).*

Ben:
Ok, now I'll I give you *all* of my apple!

(Tom walks away munching the apple whilst Ben busily starts to painting).

PUSS IN BOOTS

(Puss in boots is originally from an Italian fable but is now known all over the world. A poor Miller sets out to seek his fortune with his loyal cat. The Miller's son is sitting sadly on a stump, trying to mend his ragged coat and a pair of boots).

Miller:
Oh, dear! I don't think anyone was ever so unlucky as I am. There are my two brothers finely set up, the eldest with the mill that Father left him, and the next one with the donkey; now one of them can grind all the corn that they bring him from the village, and the other can cart the meal round; but they haven't any use for me, because Father left me nothing but his cat. Of course, it's a very good- natured cat, and can talk, too, which is more than most cats can do, but I don't see how it's going to get me a living, as he said it would do. And my brothers won't even give me any new clothes – only old meal-bags to patch my coat with. Oh, dear! *(Puss bounds in, rubs against the Miller's Son)* Well, Puss, what are we going to do to earn our living?

Puss:
Is that all that is worrying you, master? Oh, we shall do well enough, never fear. Supposing we set out to seek our fortunes together?

Miller:
What, in this coat?

Puss:
H'm, there isn't much coat left, is there? Never you mind, dear master, leave everything to me, and I'll make your fortune somehow.

Miller:
Why, what can you do, poor Puss?

Puss:
Aha! You'll see what I can do. Just give me a bag, and a pair of boots to save my feet from thorns –

Miller:
Boots?

Puss:
Yes, there's that pair you've out grown – you were trying to stretch them just now, but they'll never be any good to you again; just put a pitch on the heel, and they'll do very well for me. And where's that meal-bag you were trying to patch your coat with? You won't be needing any more patches for it –

Miller:
What do you want it for?

Puss:
But you will patch those boots for me, won't you, master? *(He takes the bag & exits)*

Miller:
(Mending as he talks). I wonder what Puss wants with that bag? He usually seems to know what he's about. Perhaps Father was right when he said he was leaving me

something better than either of my brothers would get. I wonder.

(*Puss comes back with his bag full of rabbits*).

Hullo! What have you got there?

Puss:
Rabbits, nice plump young rabbits. I snared them as they were playing outside their burrows. Have you mended that hole, master?

(The *Miller's son hands him the boots & he puts them on*)

Oh, well done! – I couldn't have made a better job of it myself.

(Strutting) What do you think of me now, master?

Miller:
(Laughing). Puss in boots! *(He seizes his paws and they dance around)*.

Puss:
(swaggering). Puss in boots! Ha! Ha! Puss in Boots, servant to the Miller's son – but you shall have a grander name than that soon!

Miller:
What do you mean?

Puss:
Just leave it all to me. And now, how about setting out to

see the world?

<u>Miller:</u>
Yes, let's set out to see the world?

(Pause to allow the passing of time as they set off to see the world).

<u>Puss:</u>
Which way shall we go – through the forest or down to the sea?

<u>Miller:</u>
I rather like the look of those hills with the castle under them.

<u>Puss:</u>
Do you know who lives there?

<u>Miller:</u>
No – who?

<u>Puss:</u>
An ogre.

<u>Miller:</u>
An ogre?

<u>Puss:</u>
He's a magician too – or so I've heard.

<u>Miller:</u>
Really and truly?

<u>Puss:</u>
All these lands are his –

Miller:
Hush! Don't you hear someone coming? Along the road there?

Puss:
We'll lie hidden here until we see who it is. Don't move – they are coming round the corner.

Miller:
Why, it's the royal coach – and the King himself inside – and the Princess, too – how lovely she is!

Puss:
Master, I've got a plan! Don't stir – not so much as a finger or toe – until I tell you. *(Puss approaches the King, bowing.)* Your Majesty, pardon me for delaying your royal progress – but I was sent by my master, the – the Marquis of Carabbas, to offer you tribute from his lands, over which you are now driving. Your Majesty, I left him just now bathing in one of his lakes, not far from here. Shall I summon him to your presence? *(Puss exits. Pause).* Help! Help! *(Re-Appearing).* Oh, my poor master! A dreadful accident has just happened to my master, your Majesty! He was set upon while he was bathing, by some brigands, desperate fellows – they tried to drown him! I beat them off, twenty or thirty of them, but I could not prevent them from carrying away all his clothes. You have more in the coach, your Majesty? *(Puss takes a bundle of fine clothes from the King, bowing as he leaves).* He will soon be ready to thank your Majesty. *(Puss introduces his master as the Marquis).* Your Majesty, my master, the Marquis of Carabbas.

Miller:
Your Majesty, I am honoured.

Puss:
(To his master). You won't forget to leave orders with me about
the harvest, will you, master?

Miller:
What harvest?

Puss:
Hush! Now, as you go along persuade the King to stop whenever he passes any reapers and ask them who their master is.

Miller:
Why?

Puss:
Because I am going to run ahead of you and tell them how to answer. And when you get to the castle, stop the coach and
knock at the door –

Miller:
Knock at the ogre's door? What are you thinking of, Puss?

Puss:
Never mind – the King is waiting – only do just as I tell you, dear master, and all will be well.

TOAD OF TOAD HALL
BY KENNETH GRAHAME

(Rat lives on the riverbank. He is talking to his new friend, Mole, about the joys of living on the riverbank).

<u>Rat:</u>
Hallo Mole! Don't seem to have seen you about before.

<u>Mole:</u>
I – I don't go out much, as a rule.

<u>Rat:</u>
Prefer home-life? I know. Very good thing too in its way.

<u>Mole:</u>
Yes, you see, I – This is a river, isn't it?

<u>Rat:</u>
This is *the* river.

<u>Mole:</u>
I've never seen a river before.

<u>Rat:</u>
Never seen a – You never – Well, I – what *have* you been doing then?

<u>Mole:</u>
Is it as nice as that?

<u>Rat:</u>
Nice? My dear young friend, believe me, it's the *only* thing. There is *nothing* – absolutely nothing – half so much worth doing as simply messing – messing about by a river – or *in*

a river – or on a river. It doesn't matter which.

Mole:
But what do *you* do?

Rat:
Do? Nothing. Just mess about. That's the charm of it; you're always busy, and yet you never do anything in particular; and when you've done it, there's always something else to do, and you can do it if you like, but you'd much better not ... And so, you've never *seen* a river before? Well, well!

Mole:
Never. And you actually live by it? What a jolly life it sounds.

Rat:
I live by it, and with it and on it and in it. It's brother and sister to me, and aunts and company, and food and drink, and naturally – washing. It's my world, and I don't want any other.

Mole:
Isn't it a bit dull at times? Just you and the river and no one else to pass a word with?

Rat:
No one else to – no one – Oh well, I mustn't be hard on you. You are new to it. But believe me, my dear young friend, the Riverbank is so crowded nowadays that many people are moving away altogether. Otters, kingfishers, dabchicks, moorhens – No one else to – Oh, my dear young friend!

Mole:
I am afraid you must think me very ignorant.

Rat:
Not at all. Naturally, not being used to it. Look here, what are you doing today?

Mole:
I – I was spring-cleaning.

Rat:
On a day like this!

Mole:
That's just it. Sometimes I seem to hear a voice within me say 'Whitewash', and then another voice says 'Hang whitewash'! And I don't quite know which of the – I don't quite know – I don't quite – Oh, hang whitewash!

Rat:
That's the spirit! Well, what I was about to suggest was a trifle of lunch on the bank here, and then I'd take you round and introduce you to a few of my friends. Does that appeal to you at all?

Mole:
Does that appeal to me? Does it? Oh my, oh my, oh my!

Rat:
There, there! You don't want to get *too* excited. It's only just a trifle of lunch. Cold tongue – cold ham – cold chicken – salad – French rolls – cress sandwiches – hard-boiled eggs – bloater paste – tinned peaches – meringues – ginger beer – lemonade – milk – chocolate – oranges – Nothing special – only just –

Mole:
Stop, stop! Oh my, oh my! Oh, what a day!

Rat:
That's all right. You'll feel better soon. Now just you wait here – don't go falling into the river or anything like that – and I'll be back in two minutes with the luncheon-basket.

Mole:
Oh, Mr Rat, my generous friend, I – I – words fail me for the moment– I – your kindness – that expression, if I caught it correctly, 'luncheon-basket' – a comparative stranger like myself – did I hear you say 'bloater paste?' – you – I – Oh, what a day! I want to stay with you. And – learn about your river.

TOAD OF TOAD HALL
BY KENNETH GRAHAME

(Adapted by A.A. Milne. The Wild Wood. Mole is terrified in the wild wood until Ratty comes to the rescue).

Mole:
(Hopefully) Ratty! (*in a sudden panic*) What's that? *(The movement stops).* Pooh! It's nothing! I'm not frightened! ... I do wish Ratty were here. He's so comforting, is Ratty. Or the brave Mr Toad. He'd frighten them all away. (*He hears the sound of mocking laughter).* What's that? *(He looks around anxiously).* Ratty always said, 'Don't go into the Wild Wood.' That's what he always said. 'Not by yourself,' he said. 'It isn't safe,' he said. 'We never do,' he said. That's what Ratty said. But I thought I knew better. There he was, dear old Rat, dozing in front of the fire, and I thought if I just slipped out, just to see what the Wild Wood was like – (*He breaks off suddenly and darts round, fearing an attack from behind. There is nothing).* I should be safer up against a tree. Why didn't I think of that before? *(He settles himself at the foot of a tree).* Ratty would have thought of it, he's so wise. Oh, Ratty, I wish you were here! It's so much more friendly with two!

Rat:
Moly! Moly! Moly! Where are you? It's me – it's old Rat!

Mole:
(He hears a voice from far off). What's that? Who is it?

(Rat appears; a lantern in his hand, a couple of pistols in his belt, and a cudgel over his shoulder).

Rat:
There, there!

Mole:
Oh, Rat! Oh, Rat! Oh, Ratty, I've been so frightened, you

can't think!

Rat:
I know, I know. You shouldn't have gone and done it, Mole. I did my best to keep you from it. We River-Bankers hardly ever come, except in couples.

Mole:
You've come by yourself. That's because you're so brave.

Rat:
It isn't just bravery, it's knowing. There are a hundred things you have to know, which we understand about, and you don't as yet. I mean passwords and signs, and sayings which have power and effect, and plants you carry in your pocket, and verse you repeat backwards, and dodges and tricks you practise; all simple enough if you know them, but if you don't, you'll find yourself in trouble. Of course, if you're Badger, it's different.

Mole:
Surely the brave Mr Toad wouldn't mind coming here by himself?

Rat:
Old Toad? He wouldn't show his face here alone, for a whole hatful of guineas, Toad wouldn't.

Mole:
Oh, Rat! It is comforting to hear somebody laugh again.

Rat:
Poor old Mole! What a rotten time you've had. Never mind, we'll soon be home now. How would a little mulled ale strike you - after you've got into slippers, of course? I made the fire up specially.

Mole:
You think of everything, Ratty.

Rat:
Well, shall we start?

Mole:
Oh, Ratty. I don't know how to tell you, and I'm afraid you'll never want me for a companion again but I can't, I simply can't go all that way now. I'm tired. I'm aching all over. Oh, Ratty, do forgive me. I feel as if I must just sit here for ever and ever and ever, and I'm not a bit frightened now you're with me – and – and I think I want to go to sleep.

Rat:
That's all right. But we can't stop here. Suppose we go and dig in that mound there, and see if we can't make some sort of a shelter out of the snow and the wind, and have a good rest. And then start for home a bit later on. How's that?

Mole:
Just as you like.

Rat:
Come on then.
(Rat leads the way and Mole trips up suddenly).

Mole:
Oh, my leg! Oh, my poor shin! Oo!

Rat:
Poor old Mole, you don't seem to be having much luck today.

Mole:
I must have tripped over a stump or something. Oh my! Oh my!

Rat:
It's a very clean cut. That was never done by a stump. Looks like the sharp edge of something metal. Funny!

Mole:
Well, never mind what's done it. It hurts just the same whatever's done it.

Rat:
Wait a moment. (*He begins scratching at the snow*).

Mole:
What is it?

Rat:
I thought so!

Mole:
What is it?

Rat:
Come and see.

Mole:
Hullo, a doorscraper! How very careless of somebody!

Rat:
But don't you see what it means?

Mole:
Of course, I see what it means. It means that some very forgetful person has left his doorscraper lying about in the middle of the Wild Wood just where it's sure to trip everybody up. Somebody ought to write to him about it.

Rat:
Oh, Mole, how stupid you are. There! What's that?

Mole:
It looks like a doormat.

Rat:
It *is* a doormat. And what does that tell you?

Mole:
Nothing, Rat, nothing. Who ever heard of a door-mat telling anyone anything? They simply don't do it. They are not that sort at all. What have you found now?

Rat:
There! (*He fetches the lantern and holds it up to the name plate*). What do you read there?

Mole:
'Mr Badger. Seventh Wednesdays'... Rat!

Rat:
What do you think of that?

Mole:
Rat, you're a wonder, that's what you are! I see it all now. *You* argued it out step by step from the moment when I fell and cut my shin, and you looked at the cut, and your majestic mind said to itself, 'Door-scraper'. Did it stop there? No. Your powerful brain said to itself, 'Where there's a scraper, there must be a mat.

Rat:
Quite so.

Mole:
'I have noticed before,' said the wise Mr Rat,' That where there's a scraper there must be a mat'. And did you stop there? NO! Your intellect still went on working. It said grandly to itself, 'Where there's a door-mat there must be a door.'

Rat:
I suppose you are going to sit on the snow and talk all night. Now wake up a bit and hang on to this bellpull, while I hammer.

Mole:
(*Sleepily*). Oh, all right.

TOAD OF TOAD HALL
BY KENNETH GRAHAME

(Rat and Mole have just left Badger's house where they have been discussing what they are going to do about Toad. Mole compares his own humble abode to the homes of his other friends).

Rat:
Talking to Toad will never cure him. He'll say anything.

Mole:
Yes.

Rat:
We must do something. What's the matter, old fellow? You seem melancholy. Too much beef?

Mole:
Oh, no, it isn't that. It was just – no, never mind, I shall be all right directly.

Rat:
Why, whatever is it?

Mole:
Nothing, Ratty, nothing. I was just admiring Badger's great big which I haven't seen lately – just comparing it, you know, and thinking about it – and thinking about it – and comparing it. Not meaning to, you know. Just happening to – think about it.

Rat:
Oh, Mole!

Mole:
I know it's a shabby, dingy little place; not like your cosy quarters,   or Toad's beautiful Hall, or Badger's great house – but it was my own little home – and I was fond of it

– and I went away and forgot all about it – and since we've been down here it's all been coming back to me – perhaps it's the pickles – I always had Military Pickles too – I shall be better soon – I don't know what you'll think of me.

Rat:
Poor old Mole! Been rather an exciting day, hasn't it? And then the same sort of pickles. Tell me about Mole End. We might go and pay it a visit tomorrow if you've nothing better to do.

Mole:
It wouldn't be fine enough for you. You're used to great big places and fine houses. I noticed directly we came in how you stood with your back to the fire so grandly and easily, just as if it were nothing to you.

Rat:
Well, you tucked into the beef, old chap.

Mole:
Did I?

Rat:
Rather! Made yourself quite at home. I said to myself at once, 'Mole is used to going out,' I said. 'Weekend parties at big country houses,' I said, 'that's nothing to Mole,' I said.

Mole:
Did you really, Ratty?

Rat:
Oh, rather! Spotted it at once.

Mole:
Of course, there were features about Mole End which made it rather – rather a …

Rat:
Rather a feature?

<u>Mole:</u>
Yes. The statuary. I'd picked up a bit of statuary here and there – you'd hardly think how it livened the place up. Garibaldi, the Infant Samuel, and Queen Victoria – dotted about in odd corners. It had a very pleasing effect, my friends used to tell me.

<u>Rat:</u>
I should like to have seen that, Mole, I should indeed. That must have been very striking.

<u>Mole:</u>
It was just about now that they used to come carol-singing.

<u>Rat:</u>
Garibaldi – and the others?

<u>Mole:</u>
The field-mice.

<u>Rat:</u>
Oh yes, of course.

<u>Mole:</u>
Quite an institution they were. They never passed me over – always came to Mole End last, and I gave them hot drinks, and supper sometimes, when I could afford it.

<u>Rat:</u>
Yes, I remember now hearing about it, and what a fine place Mole End was.

<u>Mole:</u>
Did you? … It wasn't very big.

<u>Rat:</u>
Between ourselves, I don't much care about these big places. Cosy and tasteful, that's what I always heard about Mole End.

<u>Mole:</u>
You're a good friend, Ratty. I like being with you.

LORD ARTHUR SAVILE'S CRIME
BY OSCAR WILDE

(Lady Windermere introduces Lord Arthur Savile to a chiromantist (aka palm reader). When Mr Podgers, reads his hand, he tells Lord Arthur, that he is a murderer. As Lord Arthur is wishing to marry his girlfriend, Sybil Merton, he feels he should commit the murder as soon as possible, so that he can move on and marry her. After some hilarious incidences, without success, Lord Arthur decides to push Mr Podgers into a river. Even then, the inquest reveals a verdict of suicide. The chiromantist is labelled a phoney. In this scene, Lord Savile meets Herr Winckelkopf, a rather rough looking foreigner with very poor English).

Lord Arthur:
Count Rouvaloff has given me an introduction to you and I am anxious to have a short interview with you on a matter of business. My name is Smith, Mr Robert Smith, and I want you to supply me with an explosive clock.

Herr Winckelkopf:
Charmed to meet you, Lord Arthur. Don't look so alarmed, it is my duty to know everybody, and I remember seeing you one evening at Lady Windermere's. I hope her ladyship is well? Do you mind sitting with me while I finish my breakfast? There is an excellent pate, at my friends are kind enough to say that my Rhine wine is better than any they get at the German Embassy. Explosive clocks are not very good things for foreign exportation, as, even if they succeed in passing the Custom House, the train service is so irregular, that they usually go off before they have reached their proper destination. If, however, you want one for home use, I can supply you with an excellent article, and guarantee that you will be satisfied with the result. May I ask for whom it is intended? If it is for the police or for anyone

connected with Scotland yard, I am afraid I cannot do anything for you. The English detectives are really our best friends, and I have always found that by relying on their stupidity, we can do exactly what we like. I could not spare one of them.

Lord Arthur:
I assure you, that it has nothing to do with the police at all. In fact, the clock is intended for the Dean of Chichester.

Herr Winckelkopf:
Dear me! I had no idea that you felt so strongly about religion, Lord Arthur. Few young men do nowadays.

Lord Arthur:
I am afraid you overrate me, Herr Winckelkopf. The fact is, I know nothing about theology.

Herr Winckelkopf:
It is a purely private matter then?

Lord Arthur:
Purely private.

(Herr Winckelkopf *exits and then returns with a pretty little French clock*)

Lord Arthur:
That is just what I want. And now tell me how it goes off.

Herr Winckelkopf:
Ah! There is my secret. Let me know when you wish it to explode, and I will set the machine to the moment.

Lord Arthur:
Well, today is Tuesday, and if you could send it off at once—

Herr Winckelkopf:
That is impossible; I have a great deal of important work to do for some friends of mine in Moscow. I might send it off tomorrow.

Lord Arthur:
Oh, it will be quite time enough! If it is delivered tomorrow, say Friday at noon exactly. The Dean is always at home at that hour.

Herr Winckelkopf:
Friday, at noon. (*he makes a note to this effect*)

Lord Arthur:
And now, pray let me know how much I am in your debt.

Herr Winckelkopf:
It is such a small matter, Lord Arthur, that I do not care to make any charge. The dynamite comes to seven and sixpence, the clock will be three pounds ten, and the carriage about five shillings. I am only too pleased to oblige any friend of Count Rouvaloff's.

Lord Arthur:
But for your trouble, Herr Winckelkopf?

Herr Winckelkopf:
Oh, that is nothing! It is a pleasure to me. I do not work for money; I live entirely for my art.

Lord Arthur:
I thank you most kindly, Herr Winckelkopf.

LORD ARTHUR SAVILE'S CRIME
BY OSCAR WILDE

(*Lady Windermere introduces Lord Arthur Savile to a chiromantist (aka palm reader). When Mr Podgers, reads his hand, he tells Lord Arthur, that he is a murderer. As Lord Arthur is wishing to marry his girlfriend Sybil Merton, he feels he should commit the murder as soon as possible, so that he can marry Sybil. After some hilarious incidences, without success, Lord Arthur decides to push Mr Podgers into a river. The inquest reveals a verdict of suicide and the chiromantist is labelled a phoney. In this scene, Lord Savile meets* Herr Winckelkopf, a rather rough looking foreigner with very poor English. *He should speak with a Germanic accent*).

Herr Winckelkopf:
Lord Arthur Savile?

Lord Arthur:
Yes.

Herr Winckelkopf;
I am delighted to make your acquaintance, my lord. It is indeed a privilege to meet one of the English aristocracy with the same interests as myself.

Lord Arthur:
I'm afraid, I don't quite follow —

Herr Winckelkopf:
You will, Lord Arthur, you will when I have given you my card. There, you read it.

Lord Arthur:
Herr Winckelkopf

Herr Winckelkopf:
That's me!

Lord Arthur:
'President of the Royal Society of Anarchists. Humanitarian Branch'.

Herr Winckelkopf:
Now you understand.

Lord Arthur:
I'm afraid not. If it's a subscription you want, I'm always willing to support a good cause –

Herr Winckelkopf:
No, no, no. It is not for money I have come to see you. It is because you and I, Lord Arthur – are brothers in blood.

Lord Arthur:
I beg your pardon?

Herr Winckelkopf:
Your object is the same as mine – murder.

Lord Arthur:
What did you say?

Herr Winckelkopf:
Ha! You need not look so frightened, Lord Arthur. I will not give you away.

Lord Arthur:
You're from the police?

Herr Winckelkopf:
No, I am the great Herr Winckelkopf. I do not work with the police. I support private enterprise. Now tell me, it is a member of the degenerate class you wish to remove, yes?

Lord Arthur:
Well, as a matter of fact, it's my Aunt Clementina

Herr Winckelkopf:
Ha, that is good!

Lord Arthur:
Yes, but you know I really didn't want it to get about.

Herr Winckelkopf:
Would you like me to tell you how I found out?

Lord Arthur:
I'd much sooner you went away and forgot about all of this.

Herr Winckelkopf:
Ah, but it is so clever. When I think of it, I am filled with admiration for myself. Sometimes I say to myself, "Frederick –

that is my first name – Frederick, how can you be so clever?"

Lord Arthur:
And what do you reply?

Herr Winckelkopf:
Oh, I am modest, Lord Arthur. I give a little shrug and pass it off.
But now I tell you how I found out all about you. Yes?

Lord Arthur:
Yes –

Herr Winckelkopf:
I have nothing in hand, you see. It is the off season for revolutions. When suddenly I see this man come out of the area and slip noiselessly around the corner. Out of curiosity, I follow him. He disappears into a newsagent's shop and

presently comes out with a copy of the Police Gazette. Instantly, I am on the alert. You ask me why? Because this man, he has not the look of one who buys the Police Gazette for legal information. He reads it with a furtive air. I watch him come back into the house – then, I go away.

Lord Arthur:
Ah!

Herr Winckelkopf:
Ah! But this morning early I am back. This time – a maiden comes up the steps. She goes along the road muttering to herself, as though endeavouring to remember some complicated message.

Lord Arthur:
And I suppose you followed the girl?

Herr Winckelkopf:
That is right, my lord, and when, at the end of her journey, I see the maiden plunge into a chemist's shop, I say to myself, 'Heinrich – 'Heinrich, there is some dirty work afoot. Go in. I go in, placing myself beside the maiden, and when I hear her ask for a capsule containing Wolf's Bane for the destruction of a mastiff on the account of Lord Arthur Savile, I know my suspicions are confirmed. Never in my vigils around this house have I heard the baying of dogs. Then I say to myself, 'Perhaps there is someone who may need your help'. So, I come straight to you, Lord Arthur.

Lord Arthur:
It is very kind of you, Herr Winckelkopf, but I really think I am capable of committing my own murders, thank you all the same.

THE IMPORTANCE OF BEING EARNEST
BY OSCAR WILDE

(Act Two is based at Jack's country estate. Algernon has decided to visit Jack's estate, in the hope of meeting Cecily Cardew. However, Jack, unexpectedly returns from London and is furious to find that Algernon is there, especially as he was planning on 'killing him off'. The two men retire into the house from the garden. They discuss their differences whilst Algernon tucks into afternoon tea).

Jack:
This ghastly state of things is what you call Bunburying, I suppose?

Algernon:
Yes, an a perfectly wonderful Bunbury it is. The most wonderful Bunbury I have ever had in in my life.

Jack:
Well, you've no right whatsoever to Bunbury here.

Algernon:
Well, one must be serious about something, if one wants to have any amusement in life. I happen to be serious about Bunburying. What on earth you are serious about I haven't got the remotest idea. About everything, I should fancy. You have such an absolutely trivial nature.

Jack:
Well, the only small satisfaction I have in the whole of this wretched business is that your friend Bunbury is quite exploded. You won't be able to run down to the country quite so often as you used to do, dear Algy. And a very good thing too.

Algernon:
Your brother is a little off colour, isn't he, dear Jack? You

won't be able to disappear to London quite so frequently as your wicked custom was. And not a bad thing either.

Jack:
As for your conduct towards Miss Cardew, I must say that your taking in a sweet, simple, innocent girl like that is quite inexcusable. To say nothing of the fact that she is my ward.

Algernon:
I can see no possible defence at all for your deceiving a brilliant, clever, thoroughly experienced young lady like Miss Fairfax. To say nothing of the fact that she is my cousin.

Jack:
I want to be engaged to Gwendolen, that is all, I love her.

Algernon:
Well, I simply wanted to be engaged to Cecily. I adore her.

Jack:
There is certainly no chance of your marrying Miss Cardew.

Algernon:
I don't think there is much likelihood, Jack, of you and Miss Fairfax being united.

Jack:
Well, that is no business of yours.

Algernon:
If it was my business, I wouldn't talk about it. (*He begins to eat muffins.*) It is very vulgar to talk about one's business. Only people like stockbrokers do that, and then merely at dinner parties.

Jack:
How you can sit there, calmly eating muffins when we are in this horrible trouble, I can't make out. You seem to me to be perfectly heartless.

Algernon:
Well, I can't eat muffins in an agitated manner. The butter would   probably get on my cuffs. One should always eat muffins quite calmly. It is the only way to eat them.

Jack:
I say it's perfectly heartless, you eating muffins at all, under the circumstances.

Algernon:
When I am in trouble, eating is the only thing that consoles me. Indeed, when I am in really great trouble, as anyone who knows me intimately will tell you, I refuse everything except food and drink. At the present moment, I am eating muffins because I am unhappy. Besides, I am particularly fond of muffins.

Jack:
Well, there is no reason why you should eat them all in that greedy way. (*He takes the muffins from Algernon.*)

Algernon:
(*offering tea-cake.*). I wish you would have tea-cake instead. I don't like tea-cake.

Jack:
Good heavens! I suppose a man may eat his own muffins in his own garden.

Algernon:
But you have just said it was perfectly heartless to eat muffins.

Jack:
I said it was perfectly heartless of you, under the circumstances. That is a very different thing.

Algernon:
That may be. But the muffins are the same. (*He seizes the*

muffin- dish from Jack.)

Jack:
Algy, I wish to goodness you would go.

Algernon:
You can't possibly ask me to go without having some dinner. It's absurd. I never go without my dinner. No one ever does, except vegetarians and people like that. Besides, I have just made arrangements with Dr Chasuble to be christened at a quarter to six under the name of Ernest.

Jack:
My dear fellow, the sooner you give up that nonsense the better. I made arrangements this morning with Dr Chasuble to be christened myself at 5.30, and I naturally will take the name of Ernest. Gwendolen would wish it. We cannot both be christened Ernest. It's absurd. Besides, I have a perfect right to be christened if I like. There is no evidence at all that I have ever been christened by anybody. I should think it extremely probably I never was, and so does Dr Chasuble. It is entirely different in your case. you have been christened already.

Algernon:
Yes, but I have not been christened for years.

Jack:
Yes, but you have been christened. That is the important thing.

Algernon:
Quite so. So, I know my constitution can stand it. If you are not quite sure about your ever having been christened, I must say I think it rather dangerous you venturing on it now. It might make you very unwell. You can hardly have forgotten that someone very closely connected with you was very nearly carried off this week in Paris by a severe

chill.

Jack:
Yes, but you said yourself that a severe chill was not hereditary.

Algernon:
(picking up the muffin-dish)
It used to be, I know – but I daresay it is now. Science is always making wonderful improvements in things.

Jack:
(picking up the muffin-dish) Oh, that is nonsense; you are always talking nonsense.

Algernon:
Jack, you are at the muffins again! I wish you wouldn't. there are only two left. (*He takes them.*) I told you I was particularly fond of muffins.

Jack:
But I hate tea-cake.

Algernon:
Why on earth do you allow tea-cake to be served up for your guests? What ideas you have on hospitality!

Jack:
Algernon! I have already told you to go. I don't want you here. Why don't you go!

Algernon:
I haven't quite finished my tea yet! And there is still one muffin left. (*Jack groans, and sinks into a chair. Algernon continues eating.*)

THE IMPORTANCE OF BEING EARNEST
BY OSCAR WILDE

(Act 1. Algernon and Jack meet up at Algernon's flat in London. In this scene, we discover that Jack is in love with Algy's cousin, Gwendolen).

Algernon:
How are you, my dear Ernest? What brings you up to town?

Jack:
Oh, pleasure, pleasure! What else should bring one anywhere? Eating as usual, I see, Algy!

Algernon:
I believe it is customary in good society to take some slight refreshment at five o'clock. Where have you been since last Thursday?

Jack:
In the country.

Algernon:
What on earth do you do there?

Jack:
When one is in town one amuses oneself. When one is in the country one amuses other people. It is excessively boring.

Algernon:
And who are the people you amuse?

Jack:
Oh, neighbours, neighbours.

Algernon:
Got nice neighbours in your part of Shropshire?

Jack:
Perfectly horrid! Never speak to one of them.

Algernon:
How immensely you must amuse them! By the way Shropshire
is your county, is it not?

Jack:
Eh? Shropshire? Yes, of course. Hallo! Why all these cups? Why cucumber sandwiches? Why such reckless extravagance in
one so young? Who is coming to tea?

Algernon:
Phh! Merely Aunt Augusta and Gwendolen.

Jack:
How perfectly delightful!

Algernon:
Yes, that is all very well; but I am afraid Aunt Augusta won't quite approve of your being here.

Jack:
May I ask why?

Algernon:
My dear Fellow, the way you flirt with Gwendolen is perfectly disgraceful. It is almost as bad as the way Gwendolen flirts with you.

Jack:
I am in love with Gwendolen. I have come up for pleasure? I call that business.

Algernon:
I thought you had come up for pleasure? I call that business.

Jack:
How utterly unromantic you are!

Algernon:
I really don't see anything romantic in proposing. It is very romantic to be in love. But there is nothing romantic about a definite proposal. Why, one may be accepted. One usually is, I believe. Then the excitement is all over. The very essence of romance is uncertainty. If ever I get married, I'll certainly try to forget the fact.

Jack:
I have no doubt about that, dear Algy. The Divorce Court was specially invented for people whose memories are so curiously constituted.

Algernon:
Oh, there is no use speculating on that subject. Divorces are made in Heaven – Please don't touch the cucumber sandwiches. They are ordered specially for Aunt Augusta.

Jack:
Well, you have been eating them all the time.

Algernon:
That is quite a different matter. She is my aunt. Have some bread and butter. The bread and butter is for Gwendolen. Gwendolen is devoted to bread and butter.

Jack:
And very good bread and butter it is too.

Algernon:
Well, my dear fellow, you need not eat as if you were going to eat it all. You behave as if you were married to her already. You are not married to her already, and I don't think you ever will be.
Jack:
Why on earth do you say that?

Algernon:
Well, in the first place, girls never marry the men they flirt with. Girls don't think it right.

Jack:
It isn't. It is a great truth. It accounts for the extraordinary number of bachelors that one sees all over the place. In the second place, I don't give my consent.

Jack:
Your consent!

Algernon:
My dear fellow, Gwendolen is my first cousin. And before I allow
you to marry her, you will have to clear up the whole question of Cecily.

Jack:
Cecily! What on earth do you mean? What do you mean, Algy, by Cecily! I don't know anyone of the name of Cecily.

THE IMPORTANCE OF BEING EARNEST
BY OSCAR WILDE

(Act 1. Algernon and Jack meet at Algernon's flat in Half Moon St, London. In this scene, we discover that Jack is in love with Algy's cousin, Gwendolen and Algernon is eager to learn more about a young lady named Cecily. He believes Jack is hiding something from him as he has found Jack's cigarette case with the inscription 'from little Cecily with her fondest love').

Algernon:
Bring me that cigarette case Mr Worthing left in the smoking-room the last time he dined here, Lane.

Jack:
Do you mean to say you have had my cigarette case all this time? I wish to goodness you had let me know. I have been writing frantic letters to Scotland Yard about it. I was very nearly offering a large reward.

Algernon:
Well, I wish you would offer one. I happen to be more than usually hard up.

Jack:
There is no good offering a large reward now that the thing is found. (*The butler, Lane, enters with a cigarette case on a salver. Algernon takes it at once*).

Algernon:
I think that is rather mean of you, Ernest, I must say. However, it makes no matter, for, now that I look at the inscription inside, I find that the thing isn't yours after all.

Jack:
Of course, it's mine. You have seen me with it a hundred times, and you have no right whatsoever to read what is

written inside. It is a very ungentlemanly thing to read a private cigarette case.

Algernon:
Oh! It is absurd to have a hard and fast rule about what one should read and what one shouldn't. More than half of modern culture depends on what one shouldn't read.

Jack:
I am quite aware of the fact and I don't propose to discuss modern culture. It isn't the sort of thing one should talk of in private. I simply want my cigarette case back.

Algernon:
Yes, but this isn't your cigarette case. This cigarette case is a present from someone of the name of Cecily, and you said you didn't know anyone of that name.

Jack:
Well, if you want to know, Cecily happens to be my aunt.

Algernon:
Your aunt!

Jack:
Yes. Charming old lady she is, too. Lives at Tunbridge Wells. Just give it back to me, Algy.

Algernon:
But why does she call herself little Cecily if she is your aunt and lives at Tunbridge Wells? (*Reading*) 'From little Cecily with her fondest love'.

Jack:
My dear fellow, what on earth is there in that? Some aunts are tall, some aunts are not tall. *That* is a matter that surely an aunt may be allowed to decide for herself. You seem to think that every aunt should be exactly like your aunt! That is

absurd. For Heaven's sake give me back my cigarette case.

Algernon:
Yes. But why does your aunt call you her uncle? 'From little Cecily, with her fondest love to her dear Uncle Jack'. There is no objection, I admit, to an aunt being a small aunt, but why an aunt, no matter what her size may be, should call her own nephew her uncle, I can't quite make out. Besides, your name isn't Jack at all; it is Ernest.

Jack:
It isn't Ernest; it's Jack.

Algernon:
You have always told me it was Ernest. I have introduced you to everyone as Ernest. You answer to the name of Ernest. You
look as if your name was Ernest. You are the most earnest-looking person I ever saw in my life. It is perfectly absurd you saying that your name isn't Ernest. It's on your cards. Here is one of them. 'Mr Ernest Worthing, B.4., The Albany'. I'll keep this as a proof that your name is Ernest if ever you attempt to deny it to me, or to Gwendolen, or to anyone else, who flirt with their own husbands is perfectly scandalous. It looks so bad. It is simply washing one's clean linen in public. Besides, now that I know you to be a confirmed Bunburyist, I naturally want to talk to you about Bunburying. I want to tell you the rules.

Jack:
I'm not a Bunburyist at all. If Gwendolen accepts me, I am going to kill my brother, indeed I think I'll kill him in any case. Cecily is a little too much interested in him. It is rather a bore. So, I am going to get rid of Ernest. And I strongly advise you to do the same with Mr … with your invalid friend who has the absurd name.

Algernon:
Nothing will induce me to part with Bunbury, and if you ever

get married, which seems to me extremely problematic, you will be very glad to know Bunbury. A man who marries without knowing Bunbury has a very tedious time of it.

Jack:
That is nonsense. If I marry a charming girl like Gwendolen, and she is the only girl I ever saw in my life that I would marry, I certainly won't want to know Bunbury.

Algernon:
Then, your wife will. You don't seem to realise, that in married life three is company and two is none.

Jack:
For heaven's sake, don't try to be cynical. It's perfectly easy to be cynical.

Algernon:
My dear fellow, it isn't easy to be anything nowadays. There's such a lot of beastly competition about. (*The bell rings*). Ah! That must be Aunt Augusta. Only relatives or creditors, ever ring in that Wagnerian manner. Now, if I get her out of the way for ten minutes, so that you can have an opportunity for proposing to Gwendolen, may I dine with you tonight at Willis's?

Jack:
I suppose so, if you want to.

Algernon:
Yes, but you must be serious about it. I hate people who are not serious about meals. It is so shallow of them.

WINNIE THE POOH
BY A.A. MILNE

(Winnie the Pooh takes a trip to Rabbit's house).

Pooh:
Rabbit? Is anybody home? What I said was, "Is anybody home?"

Rabbit:
No!

Pooh:
Bother! Isn't there anybody at all?

Rabbit:
Nobody!

Pooh:
There must be somebody there – because somebody said "nobody" – Hello. Could you kindly tell me where Rabbit is?

Rabbit:
He's gone to see his friend, Pooh Bear.

Pooh:
But this is me! Pooh.

Rabbit:
Oh well, then – come in.
It IS you. I'm glad.

Pooh:
Who did you think it was?

Rabbit:
Well, you know how it is lately – you can't be too careful – can't have just anybody coming in…

Pooh:
Piglet's got to be rescued from Kanga. And I can't seem to do it alone. So, if you'll come with me –

Rabbit:
Right now?

Pooh:
You DO like to take action, don't you?

Rabbit:
Certainly!

Pooh:
Owl and Eeyore won't do anything. They're afraid of her –

Rabbit:
A-ha!

Pooh:
Not like YOU –

Rabbit:
Not at all!

Pooh:
So, let's go right now.

Rabbit:
Ah – Pooh?

Pooh:
We don't want to waste time –

Rabbit:
Wait a moment. I nearly forgot —

Pooh:
What?

Rabbit:
Lunch.

Pooh:
No time for that —

Rabbit:
Imagine my forgetting to eat lunch. Won't you join me?

Pooh:
No, no!

Rabbit:
Fancy — I didn't know I had all this honey.

Pooh:
But Piglet —

Rabbit:
Nearly a full pot, wouldn't you say?

Pooh:
Honey...

Rabbit:
Help yourself. Or would you prefer marmalade?

Pooh:
Both!

Rabbit:
Here we are.

Pooh:
I really shouldn't – take the time – must rescue Piglet.

Rabbit:
One does better at rescuing after a bite to eat.

Pooh:
Much better.

Rabbit:
One needs strength.

Pooh:
I DO feel stronger! And now.

Rabbit:
Have some more.

Pooh:
There isn't any more.

Rabbit:
I have another, someplace.

Pooh:
No, thank you – I really couldn't.

Rabbit:
Just a nibble?

BOY/GIRL DUOLOGUES

WINNIE THE POOH
BY A.A. MILNE

*(Pooh decides to rescue his friend Piglet. Kanga is trying to take Piglet home to give Piglet a bath. Pooh, very heroically, decides
to take Piglet's place).*

<u>Kanga</u>:
What do YOU want?

<u>Pooh</u>:
I'm going with you!

<u>Kanga</u>:
You? You most certainly are not!

<u>Pooh</u>:
Oh, dear me –

<u>Kanga</u>:
Nasty, dirty creature! Come, Piglet.

<u>Pooh</u>:
Wait! You're right. I AM dirty –

<u>Kanga</u>:
At least you admit it.

<u>Pooh</u>:
Maybe you don't know how VERY dirty –

<u>Kanga</u>:
Tsk, tsk – Heavens!

<u>Pooh</u>:
Aren't they terrible? And just see –

Kanga:
My WORD!

Pooh:
And the teeth – (*he shows his teeth*) – Ahhhh!

Kanga:
Ee-ee-ee-ee!

Pooh:
They've never been brushed.

Kanga:
Never?

Pooh:
And my fur – full of burrs, and snarls –

Kanga:
A good combing! Wouldn't I love to go over you with a steel comb –

Pooh:
You would?

Kanga:
And then a bath –

Pooh:
Yes. A bath. When shall we begin?

Kanga:
What?

Pooh:
Well, you just said …

Kanga:
I'd love to. But what with Roo feeling sick – and I can't

neglect Piglet!

<u>Pooh</u>:
Oh, Piglet could go home. You'd have ME!

<u>Kanga</u>:
Piglet go home? But I'm *fond* of Piglet. I doubt if I could get very fond of *you*. I can't resist a challenge however – I've never seen ANYTHING so dirty!

<u>Pooh</u>:
Oh, no – not that -

<u>Kanga</u>:
(Kanga attempts to give Pooh some medicine).
Come here – Pooh! You haven't tasted it yet. How do you know you won't like it?

<u>Pooh</u>:
Just – one spoonful?

<u>Kanga</u>:
One!

<u>Pooh</u>:
All right. A strange thing – it tasted like – honey!

<u>Kanga</u>:
Naturally! Honey is one of the ingredients.

<u>Pooh</u>:
It is?

<u>Kanga</u>:
You see, honey is very strengthening.

<u>Pooh</u>:
I've always thought so! Could I please have another?

<u>Kanga</u>:
It's good for you!

<u>Pooh</u>:
An unusual sort of honey- but just the same

<u>Kanga</u>:
What are you doing? You needn't drink it all. Think of Baby Roo – He needs to be strengthened too. Give me that bottle!

<u>Pooh</u>:
Ah-h-h-h.

<u>Kanga</u>:
Empty!

<u>Pooh</u>:
I don't suppose you have any – more?

<u>Kanga</u>:
No! At any rate, *you're* not going to have any more Stay where you are!

<u>Pooh</u>:
Aren't I supposed to go with you?

<u>Kanga</u>:
I'm sorry. I'd like to take care of you – and all the rest of them – but I have Roo to think of. I can't do *everything*. A whole bottle – my word indeed!

<u>Pooh</u>:
Oh Bother!

WINNIE THE POOH
BY A.A. MILNE

(Kanga and Roo have recently moved to the wood. Kanga is a very fussy mother and is over protective of her baby, Roo. Kanga is always fussing and cleaning. Roo, on the other hand, just wants to make friends).

<u>Kanga:</u>
Well! Disgraceful! Perfectly disgraceful!

<u>Roo:</u>
Mama, can I go play with them?

<u>Kanga:</u>
Certainly not!

<u>Roo:</u>
But you said when we came to the forest, I'd have someone to
play with. And I haven't seen anybody but them. Maybe nobody
else lives here!

<u>Kanga:</u>
Nonsense. There are plenty of animals in the forest.

<u>Roo:</u>
Then, where are they?

<u>Kanga:</u>
I simply can't understand it. But never mind – you wouldn't want
to play with those two filthy creatures –

<u>Roo:</u>
Well …

<u>Kanga</u>:
Looking as if they never had a bath in their lives!

<u>Roo</u>:
Darn it!

<u>Kanga</u>:
What did you say?

<u>Roo</u>:
Nothing.

<u>Kanga</u>:
I heard it, Roo. And you know what that means. When our mouth says ugly things, we must wash it. Mustn't we, Roo! There we are – My goodness, what did you do to your knee?
A nasty scratch, dear. We'll have to put something on it.

<u>Roo</u>:
Wow-w-w….

<u>Kanga</u>:
We don't want to get it infected, do we?

<u>Roo</u>:
Not IODINE! Not …

<u>Kanga</u>:
Just a touch –

<u>Roo</u>:
Ouch!

<u>Kanga</u>:
There's a brave little Roo. Think how lucky you are. You wouldn't want to be like *those* creatures – with no one to look after you properly. Aren't you thankful? What was that?

(She spots Piglet).

<u>Roo:</u>
I am thankful!

<u>Kanga:</u>
If only something could be done for them. If I could just get hold of them for one day –

<u>Roo:</u>
Would they have a bath?

<u>Kanga:</u>
Plenty of soap and good hot water –

<u>Roo:</u>
Then could I play with them?

<u>Kanga:</u>
After a touch of disinfectant powder.

<u>Roo:</u>
Would they have oatmeal for breakfast?

<u>Kanga:</u>
And a big spoonful of Strengthening Medicine – Oh, the things
I could do with them!

<u>Roo:</u>
Would they be thankful, too?

<u>Kanga:</u>
Perhaps not at first. Not right away. But no use thinking about it. I couldn't take care of all the animals in the forest, wherever they are!

<u>Roo:</u>
How about just one?

<u>Kanga:</u>
Dear, little Roo – we'll see.

<u>Roo:</u>
One that's my own size. It would be so nice.

<u>Kanga:</u>
Maybe we can arrange for you to have a playmate. I think this will do nicely.

<u>Roo:</u>
What will?

<u>Kanga:</u>
For our new home.

<u>Roo:</u>
Are we going to live here?

<u>Kanga:</u>
Let's see … It has shade – privacy – plenty of water in that stream…

<u>Roo:</u>
Here's a caterpillar!

<u>Kanga:</u>
Goodness, don't touch! If you touch it, you'll need a bath. And there's so much to do, what with sweeping this place out – and getting settled –

<u>Roo:</u>
Mama –

<u>Kanga:</u>
Don't bother me now, dear.

<u>Roo:</u>
Somebody's coming!

<u>Kanga:</u>
Really?

<u>Roo:</u>
I hear them – and that means somebody lives in the forest!

<u>Kanga:</u>
Then stay near me, Roo.

<u>Roo:</u>
What?

<u>Kanga:</u>
One must be patient, and explain everything … Because if they *see* you, they'll *know* we live here. And if they know we *live* here, I shall have to invite them to tea. And, I don't want to have company yet, because everything is a mess!

THE UGLY DUCKLING
BY A.A. MILNE

(The handsome Prince Simon woos the Princess Camilla).

Princess:
Well!

Prince:
Oh, Hello!

Princess:
Who are you, and how did you get here?

Prince:
Well, that's a rather long story. Couldn't we sit down? You could sit here if you liked, but it isn't very comfortable.

Princess:
That is the King's Throne. Thrones are not meant to be comfortable.

Prince:
Well, I don't know if they're meant to be, but they certainly aren't.

Princess:
Why were you sitting on the King's Throne, and who are you?

Prince:
My name is Carlo.

Princess:
Mine is Dulcibella.

Prince:
Good. And now couldn't we sit down?

Princess: *(The Prince sits down).*
You may sit here, if you like. Why are you so tired?

Prince:
I've been taking very strenuous exercise. You see, I'm attendant on Prince Simon, who is visiting here.

Princess:
Oh? I'm attendant on Her Royal Highness.

Prince:
Then you know what he's here for.

Princess:
Yes.

Prince:
She's very beautiful, I hear.

Princess:
Did you hear that? Where have you been lately?

Prince:
Travelling in distant lands – with Prince Simon.

Princess:
Ah! All the same, I don't understand. Is Prince Simon in the Palace now? The drawbridge can't be down yet!

Prince:
I don't suppose it is. *And* what a noise it makes coming down!

Princess:
Isn't it terrible?

Prince:
I couldn't stand it anymore. I just had to get away That's why I'm here.

Princess:
But how?

Prince:
Well, there's only one way, isn't there? That beech tree, and then a swing and a grab for the battlements, and don't ask me
to remember it all – (*He shudders*).

Princess:
You mean you came across the moat by the beech tree?

Prince:
Yes. I got so tired of hanging about.

Princess:
But it's terribly dangerous! It's different for me because I'm used to it. Besides, I'm so much lighter.

Prince:
You don't mean that you - And I thought I was a brave man! At least, I did until five minutes ago, and now I don't again.

Princess:
Oh, but you are! And I think it's wonderful to do it straight off the first time.

Prince:
Well, you did.

Princess:
Oh no, not the first time. When I was a child.

Prince:
You mean that you crashed?

Princess:
Well, you only fall into the moat.

Prince:
Only! Can you swim?

Princess:
Of course.

Prince:
So, you swam to the castle walls, and yelled for help, and they fished you out and walloped you. And next day you tried again. Well, if that isn't pluck –

Princess:
Of course, I didn't. I swam back and did it at once; I mean I tried again at once. It wasn't until the third time that I actually did it. You see, I was afraid I might lose my nerve. There a way of getting over from this side, too; a tree grows out from the wall and you jump into another tree – I don't think it's quite so easy.

Prince:
Not quite so easy. Good. You must show me. Perhaps it might be as well if you taught me how to swim first. I've often heard about swimming, but never –

Princess:
You can't swim?

Prince:
No. Don't look so surprised. There are a lot of other things which I can't do. I'll tell you about them as soon as you have a couple of years to spare.

Princess:
You can't swim and yet you crossed by the beech-tree! And you're ever so much heavier than I am! Now who's brave?

Prince:
You keep talking about how light you are. I must see if

there's anything in it. You're right, Dulcibella. I could hold you here forever. You're very lovely. Do you know how lovely you are? I exaggerated when I said I could hold you forever. When you've been hanging by the arms for ten minutes over a very deep moat, wondering if it's too late to learn how to swim – what I meant was that I should like to hold you forever. Why did you laugh?

Princess:
Oh, well, it was a little private joke of mine.

Prince:
If it comes to that, I've got a private joke too. Let's exchange them.

Princess:
Mine's very private. One other woman in the whole world knows, and that's all.

Prince:
Mine's just as private. Only one other man knows, and that's all.

Princess:
What fun. I love secrets ... Well, here's mine. When I was born, one of my godmothers promised that I should be very beautiful.

Prince:
How right she was.

Princess:
But the other
one said this:

I give you with this kiss
A wedding-day surprise.
Where ignorance is bliss, '

Tis folly to be wise.

And nobody knew what it meant. And I grew up very plain. And then, when I was about ten, I met my godmother in the forest one day. It was my tenth birthday. Nobody knows this – except you. Except us. And she told me what her gift meant. It meant that I was beautiful – but everybody else was to go on being ignorant, and thinking me plain, until my wedding day. Because, she said, she didn't want me to grow up spoilt and wilful and vain, as I should have done if everybody had always been saying how beautiful I was; and the best thing in the world, she said, was to be quite sure of yourself, but not to expect admiration from other people. So ever since then, my mirror has told me I'm beautiful, and everybody thinks me ugly, and I get a lot of fun out of it.

Prince:
Well, I can only say that your godmother was very, very wise.

Princess:
And now tell me your secret.

Prince:
It isn't such a pretty one. You see, Prince Simon was going to woo Princess Camilla, and he'd heard that she was beautiful and haughty – all you would have been if your godmother hadn't been so wise. And being a very ordinary-looking fellow himself, he was afraid she wouldn't think much of him, so he suggested to one of his attendants, a man called Carlo, of extremely attractive appearance, that he should pretend to be the Prince, and win the Princess' hand; and then at the last moment they would change places –

Princess:
How would they do that?

Prince:
The Prince was going to have been married in full armour – With his visor down.

Princess:
Oh, what fun!

Prince:
I've got another secret up my sleeve. Very well … I am not Carlo. I am Simon!

Princess:
I know.

Prince:
How did you know?

Princess:
Well, you told me.

Prince:
I thought I was being profoundly original.

Princess:
Oh, no! Now, I'll tell you my secret. Then at this very moment your man Carlo is declaring his passionate love for my maid, Dulcibella. That, I think is funny. By the way, I don't know if you heard, but I said, or as good as said, that I am the Princess Camilla. You see, when you lifted me up before, you said, 'You're very lovely' and my godmother said that the first person to whom I would seem lovely to was the man I should marry; so, I knew then that you were Simon and I should marry you.

Prince:
I knew directly I saw you that I should marry you, even if you were Dulcibella. By the way, which of you am I marrying?

Princess:
When she lifts her veil, it will be Camilla. Until then it will be Dulcibella.

Prince:
Then good-bye, Camilla, until you lift your veil.

Princess:
Good-bye Simon, until you raise your visor.

PETER PAN
BY J.M BARRIE

(Peter Pan has flown in through the window of the Darling family's house. He is crying and Wendy tries to comfort him. She mends his broken shadow and Peter asks him to go with him to Neverland to meet the Lost Boys).

<u>Wendy</u>:
Boy, why are you crying?

<u>Peter</u>:
What is your name?

<u>Wendy</u>:
Wendy Moira Angela Darling. What is yours?

<u>Peter</u>:
Peter Pan.

<u>Wendy</u>:
Is that all?

<u>Peter</u>:
Yes.

<u>Wendy</u>:
Where do you live?

<u>Peter</u>:
Second to the right and then straight on till morning.

<u>Wendy</u>:
What a funny address!

<u>Peter</u>:
No, it isn't.

<u>Wendy</u>:
I mean, is that what they put on letters?

<u>Peter</u>:
Don't get any letters.

<u>Wendy</u>:
But your mother gets letters?

<u>Peter</u>:
Don't have a mother.

<u>Wendy</u>:
Peter!

<u>Peter</u>:
You mustn't touch me.

<u>Wendy</u>:
Why?

<u>Peter</u>:
No one must ever touch me.

<u>Wendy</u>:
Why?

<u>Peter</u>:
I don't know.

<u>Wendy</u>:
No wonder you were crying.

<u>Peter</u>:
I wasn't crying. But I can't get my shadow to stick on.

<u>Wendy</u>:
It has come off! How awful. Peter, you have been trying to stick it on with soap!

Peter:
Well then?

Wendy:
It must be sewn on.

Peter:
What is 'sewn'?

Wendy:
I will sew it on for you, my little man. But we must have more light.
I daresay it will hurt a little.

Peter:
I never cry. *(Peter tests out his shadow).* It isn't quite itself yet.

Wendy:
Perhaps I should have ironed it.

Peter:
(dancing & crowing like a cockerel) Wendy, look! Oh, the cleverness of me!

Wendy:
You're conceited. Of course, I did nothing!

Peter:
You did a little.

Wendy:
A little?

Peter:
I can't help crowing when I'm pleased with myself. One girl is worth more than twenty boys.

<u>Wendy</u>:
Peter, how old are you?

<u>Peter</u>:
I don't know, but quite young, Wendy. I ran away the day I was born.

<u>Wendy</u>:
Ran away, why?

<u>Peter</u>:
Because I heard Father and Mother talking of what I was to be when I became a man. I want always to be a little boy and to have fun; so, I ran away to Kensington Gardens and lived a long time among the fairies.

<u>Wendy</u>:
You know fairies, Peter!

<u>Peter</u>:
One came with me. I can't think where she has gone. Tinker Bell, Tink, where are you?

<u>Wendy</u>:
Peter, you don't mean to tell me that there is a fairy in this room!

<u>Peter</u>:
You don't hear anything, do you?

<u>Wendy</u>:
I hear – the only sound I hear is like a tinkle of bells.

<u>Peter</u>:
That is the fairy language.

<u>Wendy</u>:
It seems to come from over there.

Peter:
Wendy, I believe I shut her up in that drawer! *(He releases Tinkerbell).* You needn't say that; I'm very sorry, but how could I know you were in the drawer?

Wendy:
Oh, Peter, if only she would stand still and let me see her!

Peter:
They hardly ever stand still.

Wendy:
I see her, the lovely! Where is she now?

Peter:
Tink, this lady wishes you were her fairy.

Wendy:
What does she say?

Peter:
She is not very polite. She says you are a great ugly girl, and that she is *my* fairy. She is quite a common girl, you know. She is called Tinker Bell because she mends the fairy pots and kettles.

Wendy:
Where do you live?

Peter:
With the lost boys. They are the children who fall out of their prams when the nurse is looking the other way. If they are not claimed in seven days they are sent far away to Never Land. I'm Captain.

Wendy:
What fun it must be.

<u>Peter:</u>
Yes, but we are rather lonely. We have no female companionship.

<u>Wendy</u>:
Peter, why did you come to our nursery window?

<u>Peter:</u>
To hear stories. Your mother was telling you such a lovely story.

<u>Wendy:</u>
That was 'Cinderella', Peter. Where are you going?

<u>Peter:</u>
To tell the other boys.

<u>Wendy:</u>
Don't go, Peter. I know lots of stories.

<u>Peter:</u>
Come on! We'll fly.

<u>Wendy</u>:
Fly? You can fly!

<u>Peter:</u>
Yes, Wendy, come with me.

<u>Wendy</u>:
Oh dear, I mustn't. Think of Mother. Besides, I can't fly.

<u>Peter:</u>
I'll teach you.

<u>Wendy</u>:
How lovely to fly!

(They fly off through the window together, holding hands).

RUMPLESTILTSKIN
BY THE BROTHERS GRIMM

(The King has demanded the Miller make his daughter spin some golden thread for him. If she fails, the King has threatened to behead the Miller. Rumpelstiltskin, a strange looking creature appears and creates the golden thread for the Miller's daughter, but first she has to promise to give him anything he desires).

Miller's Daughter:
Oh, what shall I do? What shall I do? My hour is nearly gone.

(Rumpelstiltskin enters).

Rumpelstiltskin:
Young woman, you seem to be in trouble.

Miller's Daughter:
Indeed, sir. I am in sore trouble. My father has told the King that
I can spin this straw into gold thread.

Rumpelstiltskin:
Well, is that so difficult?

Miller's Daughter:
Oh, sir, do you mean that you can do it?

Rumpelstiltskin:
What will you give me if I do it for you?

Miller's Daughter:
Anything I have in the world – my necklace of beads, or my little speckled cock and his three hens.

Rumpelstiltskin:
(Sitting down to the spinning wheel).
You say that you will give me *anything* that I ask you for – is that a bargain?

Miller's Daughter:
With all my heart!

(Rumpelstiltskin begins to spin and produce golden thread).

Rumpelstiltskin:
When you become queen, will you give me your first child?

Miller's Daughter:
Kind sir, that would be no fair bargain for you – I shall never be a queen.

Rumpelstiltskin:
It is all that I ask. In a year and a day, you shall pay me for my work.

(Rumpelstiltskin rises and shows her the heap of gold thread).

Miller's Daughter:
What should I have done if you had not befriended me? Please tell me your name, so that I may thank you –

Rumpelstiltskin:
(stamping angrily). My name? Never!

(The Miller's daughter is frightened. Rumpelstiltskin exits quickly).

TOAD OF TOAD HALL
ADAPTED BY A.A. MILNE

(Toad is in jail for stealing a motor-car. Phoebe, the Jailer's daughter, brings him his breakfast).

Phoebe:
Good Morning, Toad.

Toad:
Good Morning, woman.

Phoebe:
Slept well?

Toad:
How could I sleep well, immured in a dark and noisome dungeon like this?

Phoebe:
Well, some do ... See, I've brought your breakfast.

Toad:
This is the end. The end of everything. At least it is the end of the career of toad, which is the same thing. The popular and handsome Toad, the rich and hospitable Toad. How can I ever be set at large again who have been imprisoned so unjustly for stealing so handsome a motor-car in such an audacious manner. Now I must languish in this dungeon till people who were proud to say they knew me have forgotten the very name of Toad.

Phoebe:
Nice hot buttered toast and tea.

Toad:
Did you say HOT buttered?

Phoebe:
Made it myself, I did. Father said, 'Here's the key of No. 87, and you can take him his breakfast. He's the most notoriousest dangerous animal in the country and how we shall keep him under lock and key goodness only knows –
'
Toad:
Did he say that?

Phoebe:
His very words. And you can take him a couple of old crusts for his breakfast, because I must starve and break his indomitable spirit, otherwise he'll get the better of me.' So I said, 'Yes, Father,' and as soon as his back was turned I said to myself, 'What a shame!' and I made this nice buttered toast.

Toad:
Believe me, girl, I am not ungrateful. You must pay me a visit at Toad Hall one of these days. Drop in for tea one afternoon.

Phoebe:
Is that where you live?

Toad:
Finest house in these parts for miles around.

Phoebe:
Tell me about it.

Toad:
Toad Hall is an eligible, self-contained gentleman's residence, very unique, approached by a long carriage-sweep.

Phoebe:
Fancy! And do your friends Mr Badger and Mr Rat and Mr Mole live there with you?

Toad:
Oh, my dear child! Badger! Rat! Mole! Excellent fellows all. They come to pay me a visit now and then, naturally; always glad to see them; but well, quite frankly, they wouldn't be comfortable at a big house like Toad Hall, not to live.

Phoebe:
You're feeling better, aren't you?

Toad:
The artistic temperament. We have our ups and downs. Any prisoners ever been known to escape from this castle of yours?

Phoebe:
Never. But I think I see a way in which you might escape.

Toad:
You're going to help me?

Phoebe:
Yes. I like you, Toad. I have an aunt who is a washerwoman.

Toad:
Think no more about it. I have several aunts who *ought* to be washerwomen.

Phoebe:
Do be quiet a minute, Toad. Now my aunt does the washing for all the prisons in the castle. Naturally we keep anything of that sort in the family. She brings the washing back Friday morning – that's today. Now you're very rich – at least you're always telling me so – and for a few pounds

I think I could persuade her to lend you her dress and bonnet and so on, and you could escape as the castle washerwoman. You're very much alike in some ways – Particularly about the figure.

Toad:
We're *not*! I have a very elegant figure – for what I am.

Phoebe:
So has my aunt. But have it your own way you horrid, proud, ungrateful animal, when I'm trying to help you!

Toad:
Yes, yes, that's all right, thank you very much indeed. But I was only thinking – you surely wouldn't have Mr. Toad, of Toad Hall, going about the country disguised as a washerwoman?

Phoebe:
All right, then you can stop here as a Toad. I suppose you want to

go off in a coach and four?

Toad:
No, no! Please! You are a good, kind, clever girl, and I am indeed a proud and stupid Toad. Introduce me to your worthy aunt, if you will be so kind. It would be a privilege to meet her.

Phoebe:
That's better. With a little trouble you'd make quite a nice Toad.

THE MAGICIAN'S NEPHEW
BY C S LEWIS

(Polly has disappeared into another world. Digory has entered the other world in order to find her. Digory finds himself in water or more to the point, under water, but he is in fact, perfectly dry).

Polly:
I think I've seen you before.

Digory:
I rather think so too. Have you been here long?

Polly:
Oh, always. At least – I don't know – a very long time.

Digory:
So, have I.

Polly:
No, you haven't, I've just seen you come up out of that pool.

Digory:
Yes, I suppose I did. I'd forgotten.

Polly:
Look here, I wonder did we ever really meet before? I had a sort of idea – a sort of picture in my head – of a boy and a girl, like us – living somewhere quite different – and doing all sorts of things. Perhaps it was only a dream.

Digory:
I've had that same dream, I think, about a boy and a girl, living next door – and something about crawling among rafters. I

remember the girl had a dirty face.

Polly:
Aren't you getting it mixed? In my dream it was the boy who had the dirty face.

Digory:
I can't remember the boy's face. Hullo! What's that?

Polly:
Why, it's a guinea-pig. *(The guinea pig has a bright yellow ring tied around his middle).*

Digory:
Look! Look! The ring! And look! You've got one on your finger. And so have I. Uncle Andrew!

Polly:
(They speak at the same time). Mr Ketterley! What do we do now? Take the guinea-pig and go home?

Digory:
There's no hurry!

Polly:
I think there is. This place is too quiet. It's so – so dreamy. You're almost asleep. If we once give in to it, we shall just lie down and drowse for ever and ever.

Digory:
It's very nice here.

Polly:
Yes, it is, but we've got to get back. We might as well leave

the guinea-pig, it's perfectly happy here, and your uncle will only do something horrid to it if we take it home.

Digory:
I bet he would. Look at the way he's treated *us*. By the way, how *do* we get home?

Polly:
Go back into the pool, I expect. (*They look down into the water*). We haven't any bathing things.

Digory:
We shan't need them, silly, we're going in without clothes on. Don't you remember it didn't wet us on the way up?

Polly:
Can you swim?

Digory:
A bit. Can you?

Polly:
Well – not much.

Digory:
I don't think we shall need to swim, we want to go *down*, don't we?

Together:
One – two – three – go. *(They jump in, with their eyes closed. When they open their eyes, they were still standing there).*

Polly:
What on earth's gone wrong?

Digory:
Oh! I know, of course it won't work. We're still wearing our yellow rings. They're for the outward journey, you know. The green ones take you home. We must change rings. Have you got pockets?
Good. Put your yellow ring in your left pocket. I've got two greens. Here's one for you. *(They put on the green rings).* O-o-oh.

Polly:
What's the matter?

Digory:
I've just had a really wonderful idea. What are all the other pools?

Polly:
How do you mean?

Digory:
Why, if we can get back to our own world by jumping into this pool, mightn't we get somewhere else by jumping into one of the others? Supposing there was a world at the bottom of every pool.

A LITTLE PRINCESS
BY FRANCES HODGSON BURNETT

(Sara Crewe is with her father, Captain Crewe. He has brought her to England all the way from India. He is going to leave her at Miss Minchin's Academy for Young Ladies, in order for her to be educated).

<u>Sara</u>:
Papa, Papa.

<u>Captain Crewe</u>:
What is it, darling? What are you thinking?

<u>Sara</u>:
Is this the place? Is it, Papa?

<u>Captain Crewe</u>:
Yes, little Sara, it is. We have reached it at last. Don't look sad.

<u>Sara</u>:
Couldn't you go with me, Papa? Couldn't you go to school, too? I would help you with your lessons.

<u>Captain Crewe</u>:
But you will not have to stay for a very long time, little Sara. You will go to a nice house where there will be a lot of little girls, and you will play together, and I will send you plenty of books, and you will grow so fast that it will seem scarcely a year before you are big enough and clever enough to come back and take care of papa.

<u>Sara</u>:
Well, papa, if we are here, I suppose we must be resigned.

<u>Captain Crewe</u>:
Here we are, Sara.

<u>Sara:</u>
I don't like it, Papa, but then I daresay soldiers – even brave ones – don't really *like* going into battle.

<u>Captain Crewe:</u>
Oh, little Sara, what shall I do when I have no one to say solemn things to me? No one else is as solemn as you are.

<u>Sara:</u>
But why do solemn things make you laugh so?

<u>Captain Crewe:</u>
Because you are such fun when you say them. Now we must go in and meet Miss Minchin.

(They enter the school and then into Miss Minchin's study. Captain Crewe talks to Miss Minchin about Sara's education).

I am not in the least anxious about her education. The difficulty will be to keep her from learning too fast and too much. She is always sitting with her little nose burrowing into books. She doesn't read them, Miss Minchin; she gobbles them up as if she were a little wolf instead of a little girl. She is always starving for new books to gobble, and she wants grown-up books when she reads too much. Please make her ride her pony in the Row or go out and buy a new doll. She ought to play with more dolls.

<u>Sara:</u>
Papa, you see, if I went out and bought a new doll every few days, I should have more than I could be fond of. Dolls ought to be intimate friends. Emily is going to be my intimate friend. Emily is a doll I haven't got yet. She is the doll you are going to buy for me, Papa. We are going out together to find her. I will call her Emily. She is going to be my friend when you are gone. I want Emily to talk to about you.

Captain Crewe:
You darling creature, Sara. Please take great care of her for me, Miss Minchin. And now, Sara, let's go and find Emily. *(They exit).*

Sara:
I want her to look as if she wasn't a doll really, I want her to look as if she *listens* when I talk to her. The trouble with dolls, Papa is that they never seem to *hear*. If, when I find her, she has no frocks, we can take her to a dressmaker and have her things made to fit. They will fit better if they are tried on. Oh, Papa! I hope Emily is actually waiting there for us! Let us go and find her.

Captain Crewe:
Dear me, I feel as if we ought to have someone to introduce us.

Sara:
You must introduce me and I will introduce you. But I will know her the minute I see her – so perhaps she will know me too. I should like her always to look as if she was a child with a good mother. I'm going to be her mother, and I am going to make a companion of her.

Captain Crewe:
My little Sara. I don't believe you know how much your daddy will miss you!

PINOCCHIO
BY CARLO COLLODI

(Pinocchio has a high fever. A Fairy approaches and gives him some white powder in half a tumbler of water. Pinocchio makes all sorts of excuses in order to get out of taking his medicine).

<u>Fairy:</u>
Drink it and in a few days, you will be cured.

<u>Pinocchio:</u>
Is it sweet or bitter?

<u>Fairy:</u>
It is bitter.

<u>Pinocchio:</u>
If it is bitter, I will not take it.

<u>Fairy:</u>
Drink it, and when you have drunk it, I will give you a lump of sugar to take away the taste.

<u>Pinocchio:</u>
Where is the lump of sugar?

<u>Fairy:</u>
Here it is.

<u>Pinocchio:</u>
Give me the lump of sugar first and then I will drink that bad bitter water.

Fairy:
Do you promise me?

Pinocchio:
It would be a fine thing if sugar were medicine! I would take it every day.

Fairy:
Now keep your promise and drink these few drops of water, which will restore you to health.

Pinocchio:
It is too bitter! I cannot drink it.

Fairy:
How can you tell that, when you have not even tasted it?

Pinocchio:
I can imagine it! I know it from the smell. I want first another lump of sugar and then I will drink it! *(The fairy gives him another lump of sugar).* I cannot drink it so! Because that pillow that is down there on my feet bothers me.

(The fairy removes the pillow).

Fairy:
What is the matter now?

Pinocchio:
The door of the room, which is half open, bothers me (*The fairy closes the door).* I will not drink that bitter water – no, no, no!

Fairy:
My boy, you will repent it. Your illness is serious. The fever in a few hours will carry you into the other world. Are you not afraid of death?

Pinocchio:
I am not in the least afraid! I would rather die than drink that bitter medicine. *(Four ghostly black rabbits enter carrying a coffin).* What do you want with me? I am not yet dead.

Fairy:
Those ghostly rabbits will take you to the afterlife.

Pinocchio:
Oh, Fairy, Fairy! Give me the tumbler at once; be quick, for pity's sake, for I will not die – no, I will not die. *(Pinocchio jumps out of bed, rushing around until he realises he is not going to die).*

Fairy:
Then my medicine has really done you good?

Pinocchio:
Good? I should think so. It has restored me to life!

Fairy:
Then why on earth did you require so much persuasion to take it?

Pinocchio:
Because you see that we boys are all like that! We are more afraid of medicine than of the illness.

Fairy:
Disgraceful! Boys ought to know that a good remedy taken in time may save them from a serious illness, and perhaps even from death.

Pinocchio:
Oh! But another time I shall not require so much persuasion. I shall remember those black rabbits with the coffin on their shoulders and then I shall immediately take the tumbler in my hand, and down it will go!

PINOCCHIO
BY CARLO COLLODI

(Pinocchio meets the Fairy for the second time and tells her that he is fed up with being a puppet).

<u>Pinocchio:</u>
I should like to grow. I always remain no bigger than a ninepin.

<u>Fairy:</u>
But you cannot grow.

<u>Pinocchio:</u>
Why?

<u>Fairy:</u>
Because puppets never grow. They are born puppets, live as puppets, and die as puppets.

<u>Pinocchio:</u>
Oh, I am sick of being a puppet! It is time that I became a man

<u>Fairy:</u>
And you will become one, if you know how to deserve it

<u>Pinocchio:</u>
Not really? And what can I do to deserve it?

<u>Fairy:</u>
A very easy thing: by learning to be a good boy.

<u>Pinocchio:</u>
And you think I am not?

Fairy:
You are quite the contrary. Good boys are obedient, and you—

Pinocchio:
And I never obey.

Fairy:
Good boys like to learn and to work, and you—

Pinocchio:
And I instead lead an idle, vagabond life the year through.

Fairy:
Good boys always speak the truth.

Pinocchio:
And I always tell lies.

Fairy:
Good boys go willingly to school.

Pinocchio:
And school gives me pain all over the body. But from today I will change my life.

Fairy:
Do you promise me?

Pinocchio:
I promise you. I will become a good little boy, and I will be the consolation of my papa. Where is my poor papa at this moment?

Fairy:
I do not know.

Pinocchio:
Shall I ever have the happiness of seeing him again and

kissing him?

Fairy:

I think so; indeed, I am sure of it. Tell me, little man: then it was not true that you were dead? It seems not.

Pinocchio:
If you only knew the sorrow I felt and the tightening of my throat when I read, 'Here lies—

Fairy:
I know it, and it is on that account that I have forgiven you. I saw from the sincerity of your grief that you had a good heart; and when boys have good hearts, even if they are scamps and have got bad habits, there is always something to hope for; that is, there is always hope that they will turn to better ways. That is why I came to look for you here. I will be your mamma.

Pinocchio:
Oh, how delightful!

Fairy:
You must obey me and do everything that I bid you.

Pinocchio:
Willingly, willingly, willingly!

Fairy:
Tomorrow, you will begin to go to school. Then you must choose an art, or a trade, according to your own wishes. What are you muttering between your teeth?

Pinocchio:
I was saying that it seemed to me too late for me to go to school now.

Fairy:
No, sir. Keep it in mind that it is never too late to learn and to instruct ourselves.

Pinocchio:

But I do not wish to follow either an art or a trade. Because it tires me to work

Fairy:

My boy, those who talk in that way end almost always either in prison or in the hospital. Let me tell you that every man, whether he is born rich or poor, is obliged to do something in this world—to occupy himself, to work. Woe to those who lead slothful lives. Sloth is a dreadful illness and must be cured at once, in childhood. If not, when we are old it can never be cured.

Pinocchio:

I will study, I will work, I will do all that you tell me, for indeed I have become weary of being a puppet, and I wish at any price to become a boy. You promised me that I should, did you not?

Fairy:

I did promise you, and it now depends upon yourself.

THE SNOW QUEEN
BY HANS CHRISTIAN ANDERSON

(Gerda has gone in search of her friend Kay. On the way, she meets a raven named Karl).

Gerda:
Everywhere I go I find the roads the same and the people strange. I wonder how many days, how many weeks, how many months I have travelled now? The snow had just gone when I left home. Then came the Spring and the flowers, and the sun got hotter and hotter, till the Summer came and the dust. The leaves are falling about me now, so it must be Autumn and ... it will soon be Winter again and I still have not found Kay. Must I search all through the cold Winter too? Now I know what it is to be really alone.

(Karl, a raven, appears).

Karl:
Kra! Kra!

Gerda:
Good ... afternoon... Mr ... Raven.

Karl:
Good ... afternoon. You aren't going to grasp for a branch and thrash me? Nor cast a sharp stone at my back?

Gerda:
Why, no!

Karl:
You are marvellously well brought-up! I am half a court raven. But Kara is a court raven in fact!

Gerda:
Kara? Who is that?

Karl:
Kara is my bride to be. She gets her nourishment from the Royal larder, real royal garbage, you understand. You aren't from these parts, are you?

Gerda:
No, I come from very far away.

Karl:
Is that why you are so downhearted?

Gerda:
No, it's because I can't find my friend who I am looking for – everywhere – a boy.

Karl:
Can I help you?

Gerda:
If only you could. You see, we lived together happily – he and Granny and I. But one day, last winter, the Snow Queen came and fetched him – and he has never been seen again. The name of the boy is …

Karl:
Kay?

Gerda:
How do you know?

Karl:
And you are Gerda?

Gerda:
Yes, I am called Gerda. But how did you know?

Karl:
The magpie is a ghastly gossip.

<u>Gerda:</u>
Then you know where Kay is?

<u>Karl:</u>
We asked and guessed, discussed and examined the facts and tried to establish, to learn, to discover where he had vanished to and to detect his moves, to track them, to check them – and not a chance of a glance! And then we discovered – Kay's in the castle!

<u>Gerda:</u>
But are you certain that it is Kay? I must go to the castle right away.

<u>Karl:</u>
I will carry you on my back. I will carry you, Gerda, to the castle.

THE SNOW QUEEN
BY HANS CHRISTIAN ANDERSEN

(Kay has been captured by the Snow Queen and is now frozen. Gerda has been searching for her friend Kay for a long time
and has eventually found him in the Snow Queen's palace).

Gerda:
Kay! Kay! *(Kay is frozen and cannot move).* Kay! How cold it is. I won't get frozen! I won't get frozen! Kay ... What is it? You are not... all frozen. Kay! Speak to me! Kay, say something! Say my name. Say ... Gerda!

Kay:
(monotonously as he is half-frozen). Gerda.

Gerda:
You can speak! Oh, Kay, it is really you! Say it's really you, say 'Gerda, I am real'.

Kay:
Gerda, I am real. Go!

Gerda:
Kay, how can you speak to me like that? If you only knew how I have walked and walked and searched and gone through haunted castles and robbers' camps and past enormous polar bears ....

Kay:
Go! The Snow Queen will come back!

Gerda:
The Snow Queen! Kay, come with me out of this icy place. Don't you remember home? Have you forgotten everything?

Kay:
I forget nothing.

Gerda:
Then you must remember – how we played together, hide and seek – and how we used to bathe in the river on a sunny day.

Kay:
Go, you make me feel cold.

Gerda:
Kay, remember home and our garret, with the stove you used to light and the rose-tree ... and Granny!

Kay:
No! I remember nothing! I don't know you!

Gerda:
Don't you remember the song or the old organ-grinder?

Kay:
I feel so cold ... What is happening to us?

Gerda:
Kay, you are waking. You are Kay again!

Kay:
I want to go home! Oh, Gerda! Take me home. You know the way. Don't cry!

Gerda:
I am happy, Kay!

Kay:
Gerda! Help me down, Gerda! Take me away before the Snow Queen comes! Oh, I can't walk!

Gerda:
You must try. Lean on me.

Kay:
I'm trying.

Gerda:
See! You can! That's it! See! Now you can walk by yourself. Come! I know the way to the palace door. The Reindeer will be waiting for us. If we can reach him in time, he will carry us away. Hurry!

Kay:
We are going home!

THE ADVENTURES OF TOM SAWYER
BY MARK TWAIN

(This scene is set in America and the players should attempt an American accent. Tom and Becky are in Aunt Polly's sitting room. Becky is returning a brooch to Aunt Polly).

Becky:
Oh, it's you, is it, Tom Sawyer?

Tom:
Come on in, Becky. Oh, I was just going to hunt you up over at your house.

Becky:
You can save yourself the trouble. Alfred Temple is waiting outside for me.

Tom:
Alfred Temple! You don't mean to say that you would pay any attention to that baby, would you?

Becky:
Alfred Temple has manners. And that's more than I can say for some people.

Tom:
He won't have any left by the time I get through with him. I'll lam him all over the place if he don't stay away from you.

Becky:
Oh, you will, will you? I guess you will think twice before you do anything like that.

Tom:
What have you got a mad on against me for, Becky? I aint done nothing.

Becky:
When a gentleman has an engagement to call on a lady and fails to appear at the proper time the lady never speaks to the gentleman again.

Tom:
Aw, shucks, Becky. I wanted to come to see you last night, honest I did, but I just couldn't get away.

Becky:
If you want me to forgive you, you'll have to think of a better reason than that, Tom Sawyer.

Tom:
Well, give me time, won't you?

Becky:
I'm not interested in anything you say or do. I didn't come over here to see you.

Tom:
You didn't?

Becky
Your Aunt Polly left this brooch at our house last night and my mamma insisted that I bring it over.

Tom:
Listen, Becky. Please forgive me. I ain't never thought so much about any girl before.

Becky:
I don't believe a word of it, Tom Sawyer.

Tom:
It's true, honest it is. Why, I'd even wear a necktie for you. If you'll only forgive me, I'll give you my tooth that Aunt Polly pulled out, and I wouldn't part with that to no one else but you. *(He takes out the tooth from his trouser pocket)*.

Becky:
I don't want your old tooth, Tom Sawyer. Let me out of here.

Tom:
I guess you'll be sorry you acted this way when I join the circus and get to be a real clown.

Becky:
What?

Tom:
You won't be sorry much, will you then? Oh, no!

Becky:
We-ell, maybe I was a little hasty but …

Tom:
Will you promise not to try to leave first.

Becky:
All right, I promise. Now what is it? Show it to me.

Tom:
And you promise never to speak to Alfred Temple again?

Becky:
Well – I …

Tom:
If you don't promise like you really mean it.

Becky:
Deed and deed and double deed, I promise.

Tom:
Then look at this! *(He rushes to the cabinet and fetches a shiny brass knob)*. Ain't it a beauty?

Becky:
Is that all you've got to show me?

Tom:
Why, there ain't another boy in town that has a brass and iron knob like this, Becky. Honest there ain't. I could get four peanut bars and a bag of popcorn thrown in for this doorknob.

Becky:
And I thought you had something real wonderful to show me. Tom Sawyer, I take back my promise.

Tom:
But, Becky, I …

Becky:
Alfred Temple has a real live pony and he's going to teach me how to ride.

Tom:
Aw, shucks, what's a pony? I guess I'll have more than one pony when I get to be a robber. I'll have a whole slew of 'em.

Becky:
I don't care what you have. Give that brooch to your auntie and don't bother me ever again. A brass knob indeed! *(She exits).*

LITTLE WOMEN
BY LOUISA MAY ALCOTT

(Jo March meets the Laurence boy at the Gardiner's party. This marks the beginning of a life-long friendship).

<u>Jo:</u>
Dear me, I didn't know anyone was here.

<u>Laurie:</u>
Don't mind me, stay if you like.

<u>Jo:</u>
Shan't I disturb you?

<u>Laurie:</u>
Not a bit. I only came here because I don't know many people and felt rather strange at first, you know.

<u>Jo:</u>
So did I! Don't go away, please, unless you'd rather. I think I've had the pleasure of seeing you before. You live near us, don't you?

<u>Laurie:</u>
Next door.

<u>Jo:</u>
We did have such a good time over your nice Christmas present.

<u>Laurie:</u>
Grandpa sent it.

<u>Jo:</u>
But you put it into his head, didn't you, now?

Laurie:
How is your cat, Miss March?

Jo:
Nicely, thank you, Mr. Laurence. But I am not Miss March, I'm only Jo.

Laurie:
I'm not Mr. Laurence, I'm only Laurie.

Jo:
Laurie Laurence, what an odd name

Laurie:
My first name is Theodore, but I don't like it, for the fellows call me Dora, so I made them say Laurie instead.

Jo:
I hate my name, too, so sentimental! I wish everyone would say Jo instead of Josephine. How did you make the boys stop calling you Dora?

Laurie:
I thrashed 'em.

Jo:
I can't thrash Aunt March, so I suppose I shall have to bear it.

Laurie:
Don't you like to dance, Miss Jo?

Jo:
I like it well enough if there is plenty of room, and everyone is lively. In a place like this I'm sure to upset something, tread on people's toes, or do something dreadful, so I keep out of mischief and let Meg sail about. Don't you dance?

Laurie:
Sometimes. You see I've been abroad a good many years,

and haven't been into company enough yet to know how you do things here.

Jo:
Abroad Oh, tell me about it! I love dearly to hear people describe their travels.

Laurie:
I've been at school in Vevay, where the boys never wore hats and had a fleet of boats on the lake, and for holiday fun we went on walking trips about Switzerland with their teachers.

Jo:
Don't I wish I'd been there! Did you go to Paris?

Laurie:
We spent last winter there

Jo:
Can you talk French?

Laurie:
We were not allowed to speak anything else at Vevay.

Jo:
Do say some! I can read it but I can't pronounce it.

Laurie:
Quel nom a cette jeune demoiselle en les pantoufles jolis?

Jo:
How nicely you do it! Let me see ... you said, Who is the young lady in the pretty slippers', didn't you?

Laurie:
Oui, madamoiselle. *(Pointing out to a girl dancing).* It's my sister Margaret, and you knew it was! Do you think she is pretty?

Jo:
Yes, she makes me think of the German girls, she looks so fresh and quiet, and dances like a lady. I suppose you are going to college soon? I see you pegging away at your books, no, I mean studying hard.

Laurie:
Not for a year or two. I won't go before seventeen, anyway.

Jo:
Aren't you but fifteen?

Laurie:
Sixteen, next month.

Jo:
How I wish I was going to college! You don't look as if you liked it.

Laurie:
I hate it! Nothing but grinding or skylarking. And I don't like the way fellows do either, in this country.

Jo:
What do you like?

Laurie:
To live in Italy, and to enjoy myself in my own way.

If you will come too. (*He bows, suggesting they dance*).

Jo:
I can't, for I told Meg I wouldn't, because ...

Laurie:
Because, what?

Jo:
You won't tell?

<u>Laurie:</u>
Never!

<u>Jo:</u>
Well, I have a bad trick of standing before the fire, and so I burn my frocks, and I scorched this one, and though it's nicely mended, it shows, and Meg told me to keep still so no one would see it. You may laugh, if you want to. It is funny, I know.

<u>Laurie:</u>
Never mind that. I'll tell you how we can manage. There's a long hall out there, and we can dance grandly, and no one will see us. Please come.

(The couple get up and dance).

LITTLE WOMEN
BY LOUISA MAY ALCOTT

(Laurie is sulking in his room as he has argued with his grandfather. Jo pays him a visit).

<u>Jo:</u>
Is Mr. Laurence in? He's not seeable just yet? Why not? Is he ill? Where is Laurie?

Shut up in his room? I'll go and see what the matter is. I'm not afraid of either of them. *(Jo knocks smartly on the door of Laurie's little study).*

<u>Laurie:</u>
Stop that, or I'll open the door and make you!

(Jo immediately knocks again).

<u>Jo:</u>
Please forgive me for being so cross. I came to make it up and can't go away till I have.

(Jo goes artistically down upon her knees in an apologetic manner)

<u>Laurie:</u>
It's all right. Get up, and don't be a goose, Jo.

<u>Jo:</u>
Thank you, I will. Could I ask what's the matter? You don't look
exactly easy in your mind.

<u>Laurie:</u>
I've been shaken, and I won't bear it!

<u>Jo:</u>
Who did it?

Laurie:
Grandfather. If it had been anyone else, I would have ... (*He gestures with his right arm in a thumping position*).

Jo:
That's nothing. I often shake you, and you don't mind.

Laurie:
Pooh! You're a girl, and it's fun, but I'll allow no man to shake me!

Jo:
I don't think anyone would care to try it, if you looked as much like a thundercloud as you do now. Why were you treated so?

Laurie:
Just because I wouldn't say what your mother wanted me for. I'd promised not to tell, and of course I wasn't going to break my word.

Jo:
Couldn't you satisfy your grandpa in any other way?

Laurie:
No, he would have the truth, the whole truth, and nothing but the truth. I'd have told my part of the scrape, if I could without bringing Meg into it. As I couldn't, I held my tongue, and bore the scolding till the old gentleman collared me. Then I bolted, for fear I should forget myself.

Jo:
It wasn't nice, but he's sorry, I know, so go down and make up. I'll help you.

Laurie:
Hanged if I do! I'm not going to be lectured and pummelled by everyone, just for a bit of a frolic. I was sorry about Meg,

and begged pardon like a man, but I won't do it again, when I wasn't in the wrong.

Jo:
He didn't know that.

Laurie:
He ought to trust me, and not act as if I was a baby. It's no use, Jo, he's got to learn that I'm able to take care of myself, and don't need anyone's apron string to hold on by.

Jo:
What pepper pots you are! How do you mean to settle this affair?

Laurie:
Well, he ought to beg pardon, and believe me when I say I can't tell him what the fuss's about.

Jo:
Bless you! He won't do that.

Laurie:
I won't go downstairs till he does.

Jo:
Now, Teddy, be sensible. Let it pass, and I'll explain what I can. You can't stay here, so what's the use of being melodramatic?

Laurie:
I don't intend to stay here long, anyway. I'll slip off and take a journey somewhere, and when Grandpa misses me, he'll come round fast enough.

Jo:
I dare say, but you ought not to go and worry him.

Laurie:
Don't preach. I'll go to Washington and see Brooke. It's gay

there, and I'll enjoy myself after the troubles.

Jo:
What fun you'd have! I wish I could run off too.

Laurie:
Come on, then! Why not? You go and surprise your father, and I'll stir up old Brooke. It would be a glorious joke. Let's do it, Jo. We'll leave a letter saying we are all right and trot off at once. I've got money enough. It will do you good, and no harm, as you go to your father.

Jo:
If I was a boy, we'd run away together, and have a capital time, but as I'm a miserable girl, I must be proper and stop at home. Don't tempt me, Teddy, it's a crazy plan.

Laurie:
That's the fun of it.

Jo:
Hold your tongue! *(covering her ears).* 'Prunes and prisms' are my doom, and I may as well make up my mind to it. I came here to moralize, not to hear things that make me skip to think of.

Laurie:
I know Meg would wet-blanket such a proposal, but I thought you had more spirit!

Jo:
Bad boy, be quiet! Sit down and think of your own sins, don'tgo making me add to mine. If I get your grandpa to apologize for the shaking, will you give up running away?

Laurie:
Yes, but you won't do it.

<u>Jo:</u>
If I can manage you, as young as you are, I can manage your old grandfather!

REBECCA OF SUNNYBROOK FARM
BY KATE DOUGLAS WIGGIN

(Rebecca and her friend, Emma Jane, have made some soap and are developing their small enterprise. Rebecca is a better salesperson than Emma Jane. In this scene, Rebecca approaches the porch of house where, seated in a rocking chair, is a good-looking young man. The man turns out to be a generous philanthropist).

Rebecca:
Is the lady of the house at home?

Man:
I am the lady of the house at present. What can I do for you?

Rebecca:
Have you ever heard of the—would you like, or I mean—do you need any soap?

Man:
Do I look as if I did?

Rebecca:
I didn't mean *that*; I have some soap to sell; I mean I would like to introduce to you a very remarkable soap, the best now on the market. It is called the—

Man:
Oh! I must know that soap. Made out of pure vegetable fats, isn't it?

Rebecca:
The very purest.

Man:
No acid in it?

Rebecca:
Not a trace. A child could do the Monday washing with it

and use no force.

Man:
I'm keeping house to-day, but I don't live here. I'm just on a visit to my aunt, who has gone to Portland. I used to be here as a boy and I am very fond of the spot.

Rebecca:
I don't think anything takes the place of the farm where one lived when one was a child.

Man:
So, you consider your childhood a thing of the past, do you, young lady?

Rebecca:
I can still remember it, though it seems a long time ago.

Man:
I can remember mine well enough, and a particularly unpleasant one it was.

Rebecca:
So was mine. What was your worst trouble?

Man:
Lack of food and clothes principally.

Rebecca:
Oh! Mine was no shoes and too many babies and not enough books. But you're all right and happy now, aren't you?

Man:
I'm doing pretty well, thank you. Now tell me, how much soap
ought I to buy to-day?

Rebecca:
How much has your aunt on hand now and how much would she need?

Man:
Oh, I don't know about that; soap keeps, doesn't it?

Rebecca:
I'm not certain but I'll look in the circular—it's sure to tell.

Man:
What are you going to do with the magnificent profits you get from this business?

Rebecca:
We are not selling for our own benefit. My friend who is holding the horse at the gate is the daughter of a very rich blacksmith, and doesn't need any money. I am poor, but I live with my aunts in a brick house, and of course they wouldn't like me to be a peddler. We are trying to get a premium for some friends of ours.

Man:
You needn't argue that point. I can see that they ought to have it if they want it, and especially if you want them to have it. I've known what it was myself to do without a banquet lamp. Now give me the circular, and let's do some figuring. How much do the Simpsons lack at this moment?

Rebecca:
If they sell two hundred more cakes this month and next, they can have the lamp by Christmas and they can get a shade by summer time; but I'm afraid I can't help very much after to-day, because my aunt Miranda may not like to have me.

Man:
I see. Well, that's all right. I'll take three hundred cakes, and that will give them shade and all. You should never seem surprised when you have taken a large order. You ought to have replied 'Can't you make it three hundred and fifty?' Instead of capsizing in that unbusinesslike way.

Rebecca:
Oh, I could never say anything like that. But it doesn't seem right for you to buy so much. Are you sure you can afford it?

Man:
If I can't, I'll save on something else.

Rebecca:
What if your aunt shouldn't like the kind of soap?

Man:
My aunt always likes what I like.

Rebecca:
Mine doesn't!

Man:
Then there's something wrong with your aunt!

Rebecca:
Or with me!

Man:
What is your name, young lady?

Rebecca:
Rebecca Rowena Randall, sir.

Man:
What? *Both*? Your mother was generous.

Rebecca:
She couldn't bear to give up either of the names she says.

Man:
Do you want to hear my name?

Rebecca:
I think I know already, I'm sure you must be Mr. Aladdin in the Arabian Nights. Oh, please, can I run down and tell Emma Jane? She must be so tired waiting, and she will be so glad!

(*Rebecca runs to her friend, Emma Jane in delight*).

Oh, Emma Jane! Emma Jane! We are sold out!

Man:
If you could contrive to keep a secret—you two little girls—it would be rather a nice surprise to have the lamp arrive at the Simpsons' on Thanksgiving Day, wouldn't it?

Rebecca:
Oh, thank you!

Man:
Oh, don't mention it. I was a sort of commercial traveller myself once —years ago —and I like to see the thing well done. Good-bye Miss Rebecca Rowena! Just let me know whenever you have anything to sell, for I'm certain beforehand I shall want it.

Rebecca:
Good-bye, Mr. Aladdin! I surely will!

BACK TO METHUSELAH
BY GEORGE BERNARD SHAW

(The Creation. The serpent talks to Eve).

<u>Serpent</u>:
Eve.

<u>Eve</u>:
Who's that?

<u>Serpent</u>:
It is I.

<u>Eve</u>:
Who taught you to speak?

<u>Serpent</u>:
You and Adam. I've crept through the grass, and hidden, and I listened to you.

<u>Eve</u>:
That was wonderfully clever of you.

<u>Serpent</u>:
I am the most subtle of all the creatures of the field.

<u>Eve</u>:
Pretty thing! Do you love Eve?

<u>Serpent</u>:
I adore her.

<u>Eve</u>:
Eve's darling snake. Eve will never be lonely now that her snake can talk to her.

<u>Serpent</u>:
I can talk of many things. I am very wise. It was I who whispered the word to you that you didn't know. Dead.

Death. Die.

Eve:
Why do you remind me of it? You mustn't remind me of unhappy things.

Serpent:
Death is not an unhappy thing when learned how to conquer it.

Eve:
How can I conquer it?

Serpent:
By another thing, called birth.

Eve:
What is birth?

Serpent:
The serpent never dies. Some day you shall see me come out of this beautiful skin, a new snake with a new and lovelier skin.

Eve:
I've seen that. It's wonderful.

Serpent:
I made the word dead to describe my old skin that I cast off. I call that renewal being born.

Eve:
Being born?

Serpent:
Why not be born again and again as I am.

Eve:
It doesn't happen; that's why.

<u>Serpent</u>:
There is a second birth. I am very willful and must have what I want. I have eaten strange things; stones and apples that you are afraid to eat.

<u>Eve</u>:
You dared!

<u>Serpent</u>:
I dared everything. And at last, I found a way of gathering together a part of the life in my body which makes the difference between the dead fawn and the live one.

<u>Eve</u>:
Life is the loveliest of all the new words.

<u>Serpent</u>:
Yes; it was by meditating on Life that I gained the power to do miracles. A miracle is an impossible thing that is nevertheless possible.

<u>Eve</u>:
Tell me some miracle that you've done.

<u>Serpent</u>:
I gathered a part of the life in my body and shut it into a tiny white case made of the stones I had eaten.

<u>Eve:</u>
And what good was that?

<u>Serpent</u>:
I showed the little case to the sun and it burst; and a little snake came out; it became bigger and bigger until it was as big as I.

<u>Eve</u>:
Oh! That is too wonderful. It stirs inside me. It hurts.

Serpent:
It nearly tore me asunder. Yet I am alive and can burst my skin and renew myself as before. Soon there will be many snakes in Eden and then death will not matter.

Eve:
But the rest of us will die sooner or later. And then there will be nothing but snakes, snakes, snakes everywhere.

Serpent:
I worship you, Eve. I must have something to worship. There must be something greater than the snake.

Eve:
Yes; I will give life myself. I will tear another Adam from my body.

Serpent:
Do. Dare it. I am the old serpent and I remember Lilith, who came before Adam and Eve. She was alone. She knew that she must find out how to renew herself and when she shed the skin, lo! There was not one new Lilith but two; one like herself, the other like Adam.

Eve:
But why did she divide into two, and make us different?

Serpent:
The labour is too much for one. Two must share it.

Eve:
Do you mean that Adam must share it with me? He will not. He can't bear pain

Serpent:
He need not. There will be no pain for him. He will be in your power through his desire

Eve:
Then I'll do it!

PYGMALION
BY GEORGE BERNARD SHAW

(Cockney flower girl, Eliza Doolittle has been taught to speak 'properly' by Professor Higgins. His aim is to pass her off as a 'lady'. In this scene, Professor Higgins is looking for his slippers. Eliza Doolittle throws them at him. She is angry. She feels that she has been used as an experiment rather than being treated as a respectable human being).

Higgins:
What the devil have you done with my slippers?

Liza:
(snatching up the slippers, and hurling them at him one after the other) There are your slippers. And there. Take your slippers; and may you never have a day's luck with them!

Higgins:
What on earth! What's the matter? Get up. Anything wrong?

Liza:
Nothing wrong – with you! I've won your bet for you, haven't I? That enough for you. I don't matter, I suppose.

Higgins:
You won my bet! You! Presumptuous insect! I won it. What did you throw those slippers at me for?

Liza:
Because I wanted to smash your face. I'd like to kill you, you selfish brute. Why didn't you leave me where you picked me

out of – in the gutter? You thank God it's all over, and that now you can throw me back again there, do you?

Higgins:
The creature is nervous, after all.

Liza:
(gives a suffocated scream of fury, and instinctively darts her nails at his face).

Higgins:
(Catching her wrists). Ah! Would you? Claws in, you cat. How dare you show your temper to me? Sit down and be quiet. *(He throws her roughly into the easy-chair).*

Liza:
(Crushed by superior strength and weight). What's to become of me? What's to become of me?

Higgins:
How the devil do I know what's to become of you? What does it matter what becomes of you?

Liza:
You don't care. I know you don't care. You wouldn't care if I was dead. I'm nothing to you – not so much as them slippers.

Higgins:
Those slippers.

Liza:
(with bitter submission). Those slippers. I didn't think it made any difference now.

Higgins:
Why have you begun going on like this? May I ask whether you complain of your treatment here?

<u>Liza</u>:
No.

<u>Higgins</u>:
I presume you don't pretend that I have treated you badly?

<u>Liza</u>:
No.

<u>Higgins</u>:
I am glad to hear it. Perhaps you're tired after the strain of the day. Will you have a glass of champagne?

<u>Liza</u>:
No. (*recollecting her manners*) Thankyou.

<u>Higgins</u>:
This has been coming on you for some days. I suppose it was natural for you to be anxious about the garden party. But that's all over now. (*He pats her kindly on the shoulder. She writhes*). There's nothing more to worry about.

<u>Liza</u>:
No. Nothing more for you to worry about. Oh God! I wish I was dead.

<u>Higgins</u>:
Why? In heavens name, why? Listen to me, Eliza. All this irritation is purely subjective.

<u>Liza</u>:
I don't understand. (*Sarcastically*). I'm too ignorant.

<u>Higgins</u>:
It's only imagination. Low spirits and nothing else. Nobody's hurting you. Nothing's wrong. You go to bed like a good girl and

sleep it off. Have a little cry and say your prayers: that will make you comfortable.

Liza:
I heard your prayers. 'Thank God it's all over'!

Higgins:
(*impatiently*) Well, don't you thank God it's all over? Now you are free and can do what you like.

Liza:
What am I fit for? What have you left me fit for? Where am I to go? What am I to do? What's to become of me?

Higgins:
Oh, that's what's worrying you, is it? I shouldn't bother about it if I were you. I should imagine you won't have much difficulty in settling yourself somewhere or other, though I hadn't quite realized that you were going away. You might marry, you know. You see, Eliza, all men are not confirmed old bachelors like me and the Colonel. Most men are the marrying sort (poor devils!); and you're not bad looking: it's quite a pleasure to look at you sometimes – not now, of course, because you're crying and looking as ugly as the very devil; but when you're all right and quite yourself, you're what I should call attractive. That is, to the people in the marrying line, you understand. You go to bed and have a good, nice rest; and then get up and look at yourself in the glass; and you won't feel so cheap. I daresay my mother could find some chap or other who would do very well.

Liza:
We were above that at the corner of Tottenham Court Road.

Higgins:
What do you mean?

Liza:
I sold flowers. I didn't sell myself. Now you've made a lady of me I'm not fit to sell anything else. I wish you'd left me where you found me.

Higgins:
Tosh, Eliza. Don't you insult human relations by dragging all this cant about buying and selling into it. You needn't marry the fellow if you don't like him.

Liza:
What else am I to do?

Higgins:
Oh, lots of things. What about your idea of a florist's shop? Pickering could set you up in one: he has lots of money. Come! You'll be all right. I must clear off to bed: I'm devilish sleepy. By the way, I came down for something: I forget what it was.

Liza:
Your slippers. Before you go, sir – Do my clothes belong to me or to Colonel Pickering? He might want them for the next girl you pick up to experiment on. I don't want to be accused of stealing.

Higgins:
You may take the whole damned houseful if you like. Except the jewels. They're hired.

Eliza:
This ring isn't. It's the one you bought me in Brighton. I don't want it now. Don't you hit me.

Higgins:
Hit you! You infamous creature! It is you who have hit me. You have wounded me to the heart. I damn my own folly in having lavished my hard-earned knowledge on a

heartless guttersnipe.

PYGMALION
BY GEORGE BERNARD SHAW

*(Professor Higgins is teaching Eliza Doolittle to speak correctly. Eliza is a Cockney flower girl. Higgins bets his friend, Colonel Pickering, that he can teach her Standard English and pass her
off as a lady).*

Higgins:
Say your alphabet.

Liza:
I know my alphabet. Do you think I know nothing? I don't need to be taught like a child.

Higgins:
Say your alphabet. You will understand presently. Let me teach you in my own way.

Liza:
Oh well, if you put it like that – Ahyee, bayee, cayee, deyee –

(she repeats it).

Higgins:
Stop. Listen to this, Pickering. This is what we pay for as elementary education. This unfortunate animal has been locked up for nine years in school at our expense to teach Milton. And the result is Ahyee, Ba-yee, Ca-yee, De-yee! Say A,B,C,D.

Liza:
(almost in tears). But I am sayin it. Ah-yee, Bayee, Cay-yee, De- eey …,

Higgins:
Stop. Say a cup of tea

Liza:
A cappete-ee.

Higgins:
Put your tongue forward until it squeezes against the top of your lower teeth. Now say cup.

Liza:
C-c-c- -cap – I can't. (*She tries again & succeeds*). C- Cup.

Higgins:
By Jupiter, she's done it at the first shot. Pickering: we shall make a duchess of her. Now do you think you could possibly say tea? Not te-yee, mind: if you ever say be-yee, ce-yee, de-yee again you shall be dragged round the room three times by the hair of your head. (*loudly*) T, T, T, T.

Liza:
Teh, teh, teh, teh … (*weeping*). I can't hear no difference 'cept that it sounds more genteel-like whey you say it.

Higgins:
Well, if you can hear that difference, what the devil are you crying for? Pickering, give her a chocolate.
(*Colonel Pickering offers Eliza a chocolate*).
Try to do it by yourself: and keep your tongue well forward in your mouth instead of trying to roll it up and swallow it. Another lesson at half-past four this afternoon. Away with you.

GIRL/GIRL DUOLOGUES

LITTLE WOMEN
BY LOUISA MAY ALCOTT

(It is Christmas time in the March household and Jo has written a play. She tries to persuade her younger sister, Amy, to perform in it. However, Amy is most reluctant).

<u>Jo:</u>
Come on, Amy … we're going to do "The Curse of Hugo' That's a fine play with plenty of dramatic action.

<u>Amy:</u>
Is that the one where I have to faint when the villain comes in?

<u>Jo:</u>
Yes.

<u>Amy:</u>
I won't do it.

<u>Jo:</u>
Oh, come on Amy … Just this once.

<u>Amy:</u>
No … all your plays are stupid if you ask me.

<u>Jo:</u>
Just this once, Amy.

<u>Amy:</u>
Oh, very well … just this once. But only because it's Christmas and I am full of the spirit of goodwill.

Jo:
Come here and rehearse the fainting scene: you always were as stiff as a poker in that.

Amy:
Well, I can't help it. I never saw anybody faint, and I don't intend to make myself black and blue all over just because of a silly old play. If I can go down easily, I'll drop, and if I can't I shall fall gracefully into a chair, even if the villain does come at me with a pistol.

Jo:
Oh, don't be ridiculous. You can't faint into a chair, it's not realistic. Look – do it this way. Clasp your hands together – then stagger across the room crying frantically 'Roderigo! Roderigo! Save me ... Save me!' Then you scream like this. Now you do it!

Amy:
Roderigo! Roderigo! Save me ... Save me!

Jo:
It's no use ... you're hopeless! Oh well, I guess you'll have to do the best you can when the time comes. Now do the fainting bit.

Amy:
I've told you. I don't know how to!

Jo:
But it's so easy if you'll only try. You must relax and let your whole body go limp, then collapse onto the floor. (*Amy tries to do it*). Christopher Columbus, Amy, that's not a faint, it's a curtsy.

Amy:
I'm sorry, it's the best I can do.

Jo:
Well, keep on trying ... Now ... we'll need the steps ... and a few props from the cupboard. Put this dress on, Amy.

Amy:
It's too big.

Jo:
That doesn't matter. Put it on ... and then climb the ladder. *(Amy puts the dress on. Jo puts on a sword and belt).*

Amy:
I don't want to. They're not safe.

Jo:
Of course, they're safe.

Amy:
I'm not climbing those steps for you or anyone else, Jo March, and you can't make me.

Jo:
Oh, can't I? *(Jo brandishes her sword & chases Amy around the room).*

Amy:
Why, you great big bully, Jo March. It's downright cruelty, that's what it is making me climb up here. If I fall and hurt myself it will be your fault, and if I did you wouldn't come and visit me in hospital ... And why am I always the one who has to play those sort of parts ... that's what I want to know ... why not Meg or Beth?

Jo:

I'm not taking any notice of you, Amy. You enjoy grumbling. Now, the scene opens with the entrance of the wicked villain Hugo and then Roderigo, the handsome hero enters and rescues Princess Zara from the tower where Hugo is keeping her prisoner. You are Zara, Amy ... so take that sulky expression off your face. Are we ready? Curtain up! ... Ha, ha! Here is the deadly poison that will destroy my rival Roderigo. One drink from this bottle and he will be dead.

Amy:

How is he going to do that without being seen?

Jo:

You're not supposed to ask that! Stop asking questions and keep to the script?

Amy:

I haven't got one.

Jo:

Just sit there and keep quiet. And smile ... you're supposed to be in love! Now exit Hugo, enter Roderigo!

Amy:

You've got a different hat on.

Jo:

Of course, I've got a different hat on ... I'm a different person. Now you've ruined my entrance! "I have come to rescue thee, my love. Let us hasten away together before the wicked villain, Hugo, discovers our plot to escape!" (*She repeats these lines*). Amy will you please concentrate? You look as though you've got indigestion!

Amy:

It so happens that I do have indigestion

<u>Jo:</u>

Amy! Now descend the ladder slowly and carefully and then Roderigo and Zara ride off into the moonlight on a beautiful white horse.

<u>Amy:</u>

I suppose you are playing the part of the horse as well

<u>Jo:</u>

There isn't any horse. Oh, be quiet and start climbing down the ladder. *(Amy's dress gets caught and she screams).* You stupid child, you've ruined the entire scene

<u>Amy:</u>

Well, I couldn't help it if my skirt has got caught up, and besides it was your fault for making me wear a dress that was miles too big. Anyway, it's a silly play. All your plays are silly and I'll never act in one again!

<u>Jo:</u>

You certainly won't because I shan't give you the opportunity!

LITTLE WOMEN
BY LOUISA MAY ALCOTT

(The two March girls have been invited to a dance on New Year's Eve at Mrs Gardiner's).

<u>Meg:</u>
Jo! Jo! Where are you?

<u>Jo:</u>
Here!

<u>Meg:</u>
Such fun! Only see! A regular note of invitation from Mrs. Gardiner for tomorrow night! 'Mrs. Gardiner would be happy to see Miss March and Miss Josephine at a little dance on New Year's Eve.' Marmee is willing we should go, now what shall we wear?

<u>Jo:</u>
What's the use of asking that, when you know we shall wear our poplins, because we haven't got anything else?

<u>Meg:</u>
If I only had a silk! Mother says I may when I'm eighteen perhaps, but two years is an everlasting time to wait.

<u>Jo:</u>
I'm sure our pops look like silk, and they are nice enough for us. Yours is as good as new, but I forgot the burn and the tear in mine. Whatever shall I do? The burn shows badly, and I can't take it out.

<u>Meg:</u>
You must sit still all you can and keep your back out of sight. The front is all right. I shall have a new ribbon for my hair, and Marmee will lend me her little pearl pin, and my new slippers are lovely, and my gloves will do, though they

aren't as nice as I'd like.

Jo:

Mine are spoiled with lemonade, and I can't get any new ones, so I shall have to go without. I never trouble myself much about dress.

Meg:

You must have gloves, or I won't go. Gloves are more important than anything else. You can't dance without them, and if you don't, I should be so mortified.

Jo:

Then I'll stay still. I don't care much for company dancing. It's no fun to go sailing round. I like to fly about and cut capers.

Meg:

You can't ask Mother for new ones, they are so expensive, and you are so careless. She said when you spoiled the others that she shouldn't get you anymore this winter. Can't you make them do?

Jo:

I can hold them crumpled up in my hand, so no one will know how stained they are. That's all I can do. No! I'll tell you how we can manage, each wear one good one and carry a bad one. Don't you see?

Meg:

Your hands are bigger than mine, and you will stretch my glove dreadfully.

Jo:

Then I'll go without. I don't care what people say!

Meg:
You may have it, you may! Only don't stain it, and do behave nicely. Don't put your hands behind you, or stare, or say 'Christopher Columbus!' will you?

Jo:
Don't worry about me. I'll be as prim as I can and not get into any scrapes, if I can help it. Now go and answer your note, and let me finish this splendid story.

THE SECRET GARDEN
BY FRANCES HODGSON BURNETT

(Mary has recently moved from India to Misthelwaite Manor to live with her Uncle as her parents have died. It is all very strange and lonely for Mary, living in Yorkshire. In this scene, she meets a young housemaid of a similar age to herself).

Mary:
(Mary sings to comfort herself). My mother was so beautiful Sometimes in silken clothes,
She came to say good night to me,
And then the door would close.
(She hears a knock at her bedroom door). What's that?

Martha:
It's Martha. I've brought some wood, luv, and will make up the fire.tha' must be nigh frozen this night.

Mary:
I've warmed up a little.

Martha:
It's not usual for her to keep a fire going' in the grate at night,
but Mrs Medlock thought tha'd be needin' it, comin' from a hot place like India.

Mary:
It's very cold here and — lonely. I hate it.

Martha:
Eh, tha' won't hate it when it clears off. And tha' won't be lonely with the birds singin' to thee, and the sheep and

ponies on the moor. Tha' will look out there beyond the garden at the moor and think what a grand place it is.

Mary:
Mrs Medlock and I drove across the Moor on our way here. I don't like it a bit. Nothing but miles of dark, bare land.

Martha:
Tha' will like it. It's covered with growin' things as smells so sweet now that Spring's comin'. And it's all purple with the heather, later on.

Mary:
Are you going to be my servant?

Martha:
I'm the housemaid. Tha' art a big girl. Tha' won't need much waitin' on. But look here, luv. Tha's got the bed all messed up. And tha' nightgown is over tha' dress! Can't tha' undress thyself?

Mary:
My Ayah always undressed me. I couldn't undo the buttons.

Martha:
Here, I'll help you – this once, mind. But you're not to have a ladies' maid. (*Martha helps Mary off with her nightdress*). There, luv. I'm thinkin' I'll bring thee new bright clothes in the mornin'. Mr Craven doesn't want thee wearin' black.

<u>Mary:</u>
I hate black things.

<u>Martha:</u>
So does Mr Craven. Black reminds him of his wife's death.

<u>Mary:</u>
Oh, I didn't know he had a wife.

<u>Martha:</u>
He did have one, but she died – a right pretty young woman she was, and he adored her. But he was always a little strange, and when she died, he became stranger than ever.

<u>Mary:</u>
How was he strange?

<u>Martha:</u>
Well, he's a hunchback, you know.

<u>Mary:</u>
What's a hunchback?

<u>Martha:</u>
He has a crooked back. And now that his wife is gone, he doesn't want to see anyone at all. He travels some or stays here in the West Wing. There's about a hundred rooms in this house, you know.

<u>Mary:</u>
It does seem terribly strange. What's that? It – it sounds like a child crying! *(The sound is actually her cousin Colin,*

wailing).

Martha:
Oh – ah – no. It's the wind wutherin'. Sometimes the wind on the moor sounds as if someone was lost out there and wailin'.

Mary:
But listen! It's here in this house. Mrs Medlock said it was the wind too, but I know it isn't.

Martha:
It was the wind. Or if it wasn't, it was Betty Butterworth, the kitchen maid, downstairs. She's had a toothache all day. Now, it's time for you to go to sleep.

Mary:
I can't sleep now. I don't like the sounds here and – my Ayah used to sing to me to go to sleep

Martha:
Aye, and my mother used to sing to me, too. There's twelve of us. I'll sing you the song I like best if you'll lie down quiet now.

Mary:
Yes, sing to me, Martha. (*Mary lies down under the covers, and Martha sits on the bed and sings to Mary whilst she drops off to sleep).*

Martha: *(singing).*
Mother of mine, where go the stars,
Go the stars, go the stars?

Mother of mine, where go the stars,
 the moment the night is over?

They put out their lights and close their eyes,
close their eyes, close their eyes.
And rest far above the sunlit skies,
until the day is over.

THE PRINCESS & THE PLAYERS
BY BARBARA WATTS

(The young, Princess Elizabeth 1st is staying with her older cousin, Anne at the Countess of Marshlake's country estate).

Elizabeth:
Fourteen times! And I still don't feel a bit better. And I haven't seen anything ... what was I supposed to see?

Anne:
Nothing silly! I didn't say you were supposed to see anything in particular. I only said that if you were tired of sitting still, you might try walking fourteen times around the rose garden to see what you could see.

Elizabeth:
Well, there's nothing to see, thank you. Just a waste of time.

Anne:
There's no point in saving your time anyway, you don't know what to do with it when you've got it, even though you are Princess Elizabeth.

Elizabeth:
Oh, dear, we're going to quarrel, I know we are, and I don't want to one bit, but if you sit there with that bit of sewing much longer, I shall... Oh, Anne, do come and play something.

Anne:
But Aunt Eleanor said we were to stay here quietly until she came back with her book.

Elizabeth:
Well, I'm not asking you to climb trees, or stand on your

head in the fountain. I only want you to play, instead of sticking that needle in and pulling it out again.

Anne:
I don't like your games. They're silly.

Elizabeth:
This one, won't be, really, Anne ... I'll be a Queen and you a courtier coming to dance with me. Let's practice that dance Master Ferrars taught us.

Anne:
There you go. You're always the same ... either you're rough or you play silly games.

Elizabeth:
Oh, dear, I'm so sorry. But it's so dull here. I'd rather be in London than this poky garden. Nothing ever happens.

Anne:
But I thought you said a little while ago that you were tired of London, that it was stuffy, and you seemed glad when Aunt Eleanor invited you to come and stay with her. I think it's very nice here, with these lovely flowers, and horses to ride.

Elizabeth:
But I do want exciting things to happen to me, and wherever I am they never do. I can't understand it.

Anne:
But what do you want to happen?

Elizabeth:
I don't know ... I want to see lots of people, to have a gay time, and dance, and have songs written about me, and watch those gorgeous players they have at the corner of the streets. I should ask them in whenever I gave an extra big party.

Anne:
I shouldn't. Those Players aren't at all nice people; they're nothing but a lot of ragamuffins, Uncle says, and he has them whipped out of the village when they come near.

Elizabeth:
What a shame! Why? Because they laugh and sing and play, to make people happy?

Anne:
No, because they're not nice people, I tell you. They're rough and they steal, and tell lies and make a horrible noise, and get drunk!…

Elizabeth:
Oh, be quiet! How do you know? You've never seen them. I have, once … at least, I had a peep at them as we rode past and they didn't look a bit like that. They looked gay, and exciting. I wish I could run away and be a Player.

Anne:
They wouldn't have you because you're a girl. They only have boys as Players.

Elizabeth:
Oh, yes, they would! I should be the first girl Player. I should wear purple velvet, and ride on a horse covered with pearls, and people would rush to the street corners to see me and shout, "Princess Elizabeth, the Famous Player … The Player, Elizabeth"

Anne:
Oh, no, you wouldn't. I don't believe they're rich people at all, for all the fine clothes they wear in their plays. If they were rich, they wouldn't … *(Elizabeth interrupts her).*

Elizabeth:
Hark! Do you hear something? *(The travelling players are in town).*

<u>Anne</u>:
No.

<u>Elizabeth</u>:
Listen. Can't you hear music? And people laughing and singing? Anne, come quick! Who are they? It isn't the … yes, it is! Look, they're laughing at me, they're laughing!

<u>Anne</u>:
Elizabeth, don't, don't! Come back! It's the Players! Don't look at them! *(Anne is horrified as she believes the players to be beneath them).*

<u>Elizabeth</u>:
They're beckoning to me. I must go out and speak to them.

<u>Anne</u>:
You can't!

<u>Elizabeth</u>:
Perhaps they'd come in here. Oh, look, they've stopped.

<u>Anne</u>:
You can't! Stop doing that! Aunt Eleanor would be furious.

(Elizabeth runs to the garden gate and beckons to them to come closer).

<u>Elizabeth</u>:
Gentlemen, I am the Princess Elizabeth and this is the house of the Countess of Marshlake. She is not here at present, but we both take great pleasure in inviting you into our garden.

BEAUTY AND THE BEAST
BY NICHOLAS STUART GRAY

(The time is 1840 and Beauty's two sisters, Jessamine and Jonquiline, are upset that Beauty has to return to the Beast's castle).

<u>Jessamine</u>:
If we weren't quite so silly, we could think of the right things to say that would keep her here with us.

<u>Jonquiline</u>:
But we can't. We've said everything we can think of. We've begged and begged her to stay … and oh, how we've cried.

<u>Jessamine</u>:
She has made up her mind.

<u>Jonquiline</u>:
And she's going to leave us, again.

<u>Jessamine</u>:
And go back to that horrid Beast, and his great dark castle. She can't like the Beast as much as she likes us.

<u>Jonquiline</u>:
How could she?

<u>Jessamine</u>:
She's sorry for him. All this week she has been worrying about him … and wondering if he is having proper meals, and staying out at night in the forest. She's very sorry for him.

<u>Jonquiline</u>:
I'm a bit sorry for him too, but not very much. Not if he takes Beauty away from us.

<u>Jessamine</u>:
And he is. She's going away.

<u>Jonquiline</u>:
Now.

<u>Jessamine</u>:
We can't stop her.

<u>Jonquiline</u>:
I hate the Beast!

<u>Jessamine</u>:
It's not proper to hate, Jonquiline.

<u>Jonquiline</u>:
I don't care. I hate him.

<u>Jessamine</u>:
So, do I.

<u>Jonquiline</u>:
I wish his horrid rose would die. It smells so sweet. Yet I wish it would die.

<u>Jessamine</u>:
Then the Beast would die, also.

<u>Jonquiline</u>:
Then … then … oh, dear, I wish we could steal the ring.

<u>Jessamine</u>:
Then Beauty couldn't go back to him, at all.

<u>Jonquiline</u>:
(She goes to the dressing table and looks at the ring).
Shall we steal it? Here it is, Jessamine.

<u>Jessamine</u>:
That would be most improper of us, Jonquiline.

Jonquiline:
It would keep Beauty here with us.

Jessamine:
And the Beast would die.

Jonquiline:
Then I suppose we mustn't steal it ... and Beauty must leave us. Forever ... Oh, I do hate the Beast and his rose and this ring!

Jessamine:
Oh, be careful!
(She carelessly drops the ring).

Jonquiline:
I don't care! I don't care! I hope it's lost! I want Beauty!

Jessamine:
But where has it gone? Jonquiline, help me .... I can't find the ring!

Jonquiline:
I don't ca ... what did you say?

Jessamine:
I can*not* find the ring!

Jonquiline:
Oh, my goodness!

Jessamine:
Oh, be quick! It's nearly ten o'clock.

Jonquiline:
There's no sign of it.

Jessamine:
Oh! Oh! Jonquiline ... it must have gone down the mouse-hole!

<u>Jonquiline</u>:
Oh, dear. Let us look.

<u>Jessamine</u>:
I can't see it.

<u>Jonquiliine</u>:
It's dark in there.

<u>Jessamine</u>:
I can't get my hand inside.

<u>Jonquiline</u>:
It's lost.

<u>Jessamine</u>:Completely lost.

<u>Jonquiline</u>:
Forever.

<u>Jessamine</u>:
What shall we say to Beauty? Oh, my goodness, what will she say to us? Jonquiline ….

<u>Jonquiline</u>:
I cannot tell her. I cannot. She'll say I'm silly.

<u>Jessamine</u>:
We must make up a story.

<u>Jonquiline</u>:
But what?

<u>Jessamine</u>:
Don't cry, Jonquiline. If the ring is lost there's no use crying. And Beauty need not know just how silly you … *we* …. have been this time.

<u>Jonquiliine</u>:
What will you tell her?

<u>Jessamine</u>:
I shall say ... now listen, Jonquiline ... this is quite clever of me ... I shall say that a big bird flew through the window and carried the ring off the dressing-table, and away out into the night again. A very big bird stole it.

<u>Jonquiline</u>:
But that isn't true.

<u>Jessamine</u>:
Well ... it's not exactly a lie. It's a sort of excuse.

<u>Jonquiline</u>:
It sounds rather like a lie.

<u>Jessamine</u>:
Do you want to tell Beauty that you dropped it down a mouse-hole?

<u>Jonquiline</u>:
No, oh, no!

<u>Jessamine</u>:
Well, you see, a mouse has really stolen it. If I say it was a bird, instead of a mouse ... well, a bird is only a bigger mouse with wings.

<u>Jonquiline</u>:
It sounds better now that you have explained it.

<u>Jessamine</u>:
It's just gone ten o'clock.

<u>Jonquiline</u>:
And here comes Papa, with Beauty.

<u>Jessamine</u>:
Now, do be brave, Jonquiline.

THE WIZARD OF OZ
BY L. FRANK BAUM

(After a huge cyclone, Dorothy finds herself over the rainbow. The first person she meets is the Good Witch of the North.
Unfortunately, there are still the Wicked Witches of the East and the West for Dorothy to contend with).

Good Witch:
You are welcome, most noble Sorceress, to the Land of Munchkins.

Dorothy:
You are very kind.

Good Witch:
We are grateful to you for having killed the Wicked Witch of the East and for setting our people free from her spell.

Dorothy:
But there must be some mistake. I haven't killed anyone.

Good Witch:
Well, your house did, and that is the same thing. See! There are the witch's shoes, still sticking out from underneath it.

Dorothy:
Oh dear, the house was blown away by a strong wind. It must have fallen on her. What shall we do?

Good Witch:
Nothing. There is nothing we can do. She was wicked and paid for her wickedness. Now that she is dead, the Munchkins are all free and happy again.

Dorothy:
But who are the Munchkins?

Good Witch:
They are the people who live in the Land of the East where the wicked witch rules.

Dorothy:
Are you a Munchkin?

Good Witch:
(She laughs). No, but I am their friend. I am the Witch of the North.

Dorothy:
Oh, dear! Are you really a witch?

Good Witch:
Yes, indeed, but I am a good witch and the people love me. I am not as powerful as the Wicked Witch was, or I should have set the people free myself.

Dorothy:
But I thought all witches were wicked.

Good Witch:
Oh no! You are making a great mistake. There are wizards too. Oz himself is a great Wizard. He is more powerful than all the rest of us put together. He lives in the City of Green Emeralds. Look!

Dorothy:
What is it?

Good Witch:
(The silver shoes are sticking out from under the house). The Wicked Witch has disappeared. There is nothing left of her but her silver shoes. The silver shoes belong to you now and you must wear them from now on.

<u>Dorothy:</u>
But they're beautiful!

<u>Good Witch:</u>
There is some magic charm connected with them. She would never let them out of her sight.

<u>Dorothy:</u>
It's very kind of you to give them to me. I am very anxious to get back to my aunt and uncle. Can you help me find the way?

<u>Good Witch:</u>
You must go to the City of Emeralds and perhaps Oz will help you.

<u>Dorothy:</u>
Where is the City of Emeralds?

<u>Good Witch:</u>
It is exactly in the centre of the country, and is ruled by Oz.

<u>Dorothy:</u>
Is he a good man?

<u>Good Witch:</u>
He is a good Wizard. Whether he is a man or not, I cannot tell because I have never seen him.

<u>Dorothy:</u>
But how do I get there?

<u>Good Witch:</u>
You must walk. It is a very long journey, through a country that is sometimes dark and terrible. But you must not be afraid. I will use
all the magic arts I know of to keep you from harm.

Dorothy:
Won't you come with me?

Good Witch:
No, I cannot do that, but I will give you my kiss. No one will dare injure a person who has been kissed by the Witch of the North. *(She kisses Dorothy).* You must find the way to the Emerald City by yourself, but you will find the road is paved with yellow bricks, so, you cannot miss it. When you get to the Wizard of Oz, don't be afraid of him. Tell him your story and ask him to help you. Now, I have to leave you. Don't forget, look for the yellow brick road.

Dorothy:
I wonder if the silver shoes will fit me? *(She tries on the silver shoes).* Yes, they do. Now come along Toto *(Toto is her dog),* we've got a long journey in front of us. Let's look for the yellow brick road.

ANNE OF GREEN GABLES
BY L.M MONTGOMERY

(Anne Shirley is an orphan who has gone to stay at Green Gables with Marilla. Anne is worried that she may be sent back as the family really wanted a boy to help out with the work on the farm. In this scene, Marilla helps Anne say her prayers before going to bed).

Marilla:
Now, Anne, I noticed last night that you threw your clothes all about the floor when you took them off. That is a very untidy habit and I can't allow it. As soon as you take of any article of clothing, fold it neatly and place it on the chair.

Anne:
I was so disturbed in my mind last night, that I didn't think about my clothes. I'll fold them nicely tonight. *(Anne & Marilla fold Anne's clothes).* They always made us do this at the orphanage. Though half the time, I'd forget, I'd be in such a hurry to get into bed to imagine things.

Marilla:
Well, you'll have to remember a little better if you're to stay here. There! That's more like it. Say your prayers now and get into bed.

Anne:
I never say prayers.

Marilla:
What do you mean? Weren't you taught to say your prayers? Don't you know who God is, Anne?

Anne:
God is a spirit, infinite, eternal, and unchangeable.

Marilla:
So, you do know something then, thank goodness. You're not quite a heathen. Where did you learn?

Anne:
At Sunday school. They made us learn the whole catechism. There is something splendid about some of the words. 'Infinite, eternal, unchangeable'. Isn't that grand? You can't quite call it poetry but it sounds a lot like it, doesn't it?

Marilla:
We're not talking about poetry, Anne, we are talking about saying your prayers. Don't you know it's a terribly wicked thing not to say your prayers every night?

Anne:
You'd find it easier to be bad than good if you had red hair. Mrs Thomas told me that God made my hair red *on purpose* and I've never cared about Him since. And anyhow, I'd always be too tired at night to bother about saying my prayers.

Marilla:
You must say your prayers, Ann, while you are under my roof.

Anne:
If you want me to, of course, anything to oblige, but you'll have to tell me what to say this time until I've had time to imagine a nice prayer to say.

Marilla:
Very well, but you must kneel down.

Anne:
Why must people kneel down to pray? If I really wanted to pray, I'd go out into a great big field all alone or into the deep, deep woods and I'd look up into the sky, up, up, up

into the lovely blue sky that looks as if there was no end to its blueness ... and then I'd just feel like a prayer. *(Marilla gives Anne a look and Anne kneels)*. Well, I'm ready. What should I say?

Marilla:
You are old enough to pray for yourself, Anne. Just thank God for your blessings and ask Him humbly for the things you want.

Anne:
Well, I'll do my best. Gracious Heavenly Father, that's the way the ministers say it in church. I thank thee for the White Way of Delight and the Lake of Shining Waters and the Snow Queen. I'm really extremely grateful for them. That's all the blessings I can think of just for now. As for the things I want, they're so numerous that it would take a great deal of time to name them all, so I will mention the two most important. Please let me stay at Green Gables; and please let me be good-looking when I grow up. Yours respectfully, Anne Shirley. *(Opening her eyes and looking at Marilla)*. There, did I do it all right?

ANNE OF GREEN GABLES
BY L.M MONTGOMERY

(Anne is an orphan. She has just come to Green Gables. The story takes place in Canada. Anne has invited her best friend, Diana, to tea. She tries to be very grown up and offers Diana some raspberry cordial).

Anne:

Hello, Diana. Thank you for coming. Do come in. Do sit down.

Diana:

Why, thank you, Anne. How gracious you are.

(The two girls sit self-consciously for a while).

Have we been dignified for long enough, do you think? Good. We can have tea now. *(After a slight pause).* I believe we have fulfilled our social duty.

Anne:

Oh good. We can have tea now. Marilla said we could have fruit cake and cherry preserves for tea. But it isn't good manners to tell your company what you are going to give them to eat, so I won't tell you what she said we could have to drink. Only, it begins with an R and a C and it's a bright red colour. I love bright red drinks, don't you? They taste twice as good as any other colour. Help yourself to the raspberry cordial, Diana.
(Anne passes the bottle to Diana).

Diana:
Will you have some?

Anne:
I don't think I will have any. I've eaten ever so many apples today and I feel a little ….

Diana:
I understand.

Anne:
Tell me about school. I can't wait to come back.

Diana:
I hope it's soon I've had to sit next to Gertie Pie. She squeaks her pencil all the time and it just makes my blood run cold. Ruby Gillis has charmed all her warts away with a magic pebble that old Mary Joe from the Creek gave her. You rub the warts with the pebble and then throw it away over your left shoulder at the time of the new moon and all the warts go away. Charlie Sloane's name was written up with Em White's on the porch wall and Em White was awful mad about it. And Sam Boulter sassed Mr Phillips in class and Mr Phillips whipped him and Sam father came down to the school and dared Mr Phillips to lay a hand on one of his children again.

Anne:
Really? I've missed an awful lot, haven't I?

Diana:
Everyone misses you and wishes you would come to school again soon.

Anne:
Have another glass of cordial, Diana?

Diana:
I will. It's awfully nice raspberry cordial, Anne. I didn't know raspberry cordial was so nice.

Anne:
I'm really glad you like it. Marilla said it was on the shelf but I couldn't find it and I had to search and search. In the end it was

right up on the top shelf. I had to stretch. My, you drank that fast. Here, have some more. *(Anne fills up Diana's glass again. Diana is enjoying it and drinks quickly).*

Diana:
The nicest cordial I ever drank. It's ever so much nicer than Mrs Lynde's, although she brags of hers so much. *(Diana drinks more cordial).*

Anne:
I should think Marilla's raspberry cordial would be much nicer than Mrs Lynde's. Marilla is a famous cook. She is trying to teach me to cook but I assure you, Diana, it is uphill work. There's so little scope for imagination in cookery. You just have to go by the rules. The last time I made a cake, I was thinking the loveliest story about you and me, Diana. I thought you were desperately ill with smallpox and everybody deserted you, but I went boldly to your bedside and nursed you back to life; and then I took the smallpox and died and I was buried under those poplar trees in the graveyard and you planted a rosebush by my grave and watered it with your tears; and you never, never forgot the friend of your youth who sacrificed her life for you. Oh, it was such a pathetic tale, Diana. The tears just rained down over my cheeks while I mixed the cake. But I forgot to put in the flour and the cake was a dismal failure. Flour is so essential in cakes, you know. Marilla was very cross. Why, Diana, what's the matter? You're sick!

Diana:
I feel sick – awful sick. I must go home.
(Diana has in fact, been drinking alcohol, unknowingly. She is feeling very sick and falls to the floor).

Anne:
Diana! Diana! Oh, what if she's dead? *(Anne kneels down beside her).* Don't worry. I'm here, Diana. I'll never forsake you!

A LITTLE PRINCESS
BY FRANCES HODGSON BURNETT

(At Miss Minchin's Academy. Sara befriends Ermengarde, a shy and awkward girl).

Sara:
What is your name?

Ermengarde:
My name's Ermengarde St. John.

Sara:
Mine is Sara Crewe. Yours is very pretty. It sounds like a storybook.

Ermengarde:
Do you like it? I—I like yours. You can speak French, can't you?

Sara:
I can speak it because I have heard it all my life. You could speak it if you had always heard it.

Ermengarde:
Oh, no, I couldn't. I *never* could speak it! Why? You heard me just now. I'm always like that. I can't *say* the words. They're so queer. You are *clever,* aren't you?

Sara:
I don't know. Would you like to see Emily? (*Emily is Sara's doll).*

Ermengarde:
Who is Emily?

<u>Sara:</u>
Come up to my room and see. (*Holding out her hand*).

<u>Ermengarde:</u>
Is it true, is it true that you have a playroom all to yourself?

<u>Sara:</u>
Yes! Papa asked Miss Minchin to let me have one, because—well, it is because when I play, I make up stories and tell them to myself, and I don't like people to hear me. It spoils it if I think people listen.

<u>Ermengarde:</u>
You *make* up stories! Can you do that—as well as speak French? Can you?

<u>Sara:</u>
Why, anyone can make up things. Have you never tried? Let us go very quietly to the door, and then I will open it quite suddenly; perhaps we may catch her.

(*They make not the least noise until they reach the door. Then Sara suddenly turns the handle, and throws it wide open. Its opening reveals Sara's room with a wonderful doll sitting in a chair by it, apparently reading a book*).

Oh, she got back to her seat before we could see her! Of course, they always do. They are as quick as lightning.

<u>Ermengarde:</u>
Can she walk?

<u>Sara:</u>
Yes. At least I believe she can. At least I *pretend* I believe she can. And that makes it seem as if it were true. Have you never pretended things?

<u>Ermengarde:</u>
No. Never. Tell me about it.

Sara:
Let us sit down and I will tell you. It's so easy that when you begin you can't stop. You just go on and on doing it always. And it's beautiful. Emily, you must listen. This is Ermengarde, Emily. Ermengarde, this is Emily. Would you like to hold her?

Ermengarde:
Oh, may I? May I, really? She is beautiful! (*Sara puts her doll Emily into her arms*).

Sara:
I'll tell you stories of India; and the dolls who walk and talk, and who can do anything they choose when human beings are out of the room, but who must keep their powers a secret and so fly back to their places 'like lightning' when people return to the room. *We* couldn't do it. You see, it's a kind of magic.

(*Ermengarde sees Sara's face suddenly change*).

Ermengarde:
Have you a—a pain?

Sara:
Yes, but it is not in my body. Do you love your father more than anything else in all the whole world?

Ermengarde:
I—I scarcely ever see him. He is always in the library—reading things.

Sara:
I love mine more than all the world ten times over. That is what my pain is. He has gone away. I promised him I would bear it. And I will. You have to bear things. Think what soldiers bear! Papa is a soldier. If there was a war, he would have to bear marching and thirstiness and, perhaps, deep wounds. And he would never say a word—not one

word. If I go on talking and talking, and telling you things about pretending, I shall bear it better. You don't forget, but you bear it better

Ermengarde:

Lavinia and Jessie are best friends, I wish we could be 'best friends'. Would you have me for yours? You're clever, and I'm the stupidest child in the school, but I—oh, I do so like you!

Sara:

I'm glad of that. It makes one thankful when you are liked. Yes. We will be friends. And I'll tell you what - I can help you with your French lessons.

A LITTLE PRINCESS
BY FRANCES HODGSON BURNETT

(Sara has been telling a story. Becky, a young servant girl has been sweeping the hearth and has been listening to the story).

Sara:

(Sara is telling a story). The Mermaids swam softly about in the crystal-green water, and dragged after them a fishing-net woven of deep-sea pearls. The Princess sat on the white rock and watched them. It was a wonderful story about a princess who was loved by a Prince Merman, and went to live with him in shining caves under the sea.

*(Becky, a servant is sweeping the hearth. The sound of Sara's
story has mesmerized her. She is so tired that she falls asleep).*

Sara:

What is your name? Poor thing! I don't like to waken her. But Miss Minchin would be cross if she found out. I'll just wait a few minutes. But she is so tired. She is so tired!

(Becky springs up and clutches at her cap when she is awakened by a lump of coal falling from the fire).

Becky:

Oh, miss! Oh, miss! I arst yer pardon, miss! Oh, I do, miss!

Sara:

Don't be frightened. It doesn't matter the least bit.

Becky:

I didn't mean to do it, miss. It was the warm fire—an' me

bein' so tired. It—it *wasn't* impertinence!

(Sara breaks into a friendly little laugh and puts her hand on her shoulder).

Sara:
You were tired. You could not help it. You are not really awake yet.

Becky:
Ain't—ain't yer angry, miss? Ain't yer goin' to tell the missus?

Sara:
No. Of course I'm not. Why, we are just the same—I am only a little girl like you. It's just an accident that I am not you, and you are not me!

Becky:
A' accident, miss. Is it?

Sara:
Yes! Have you done your work? Dare you stay here a few minutes?

Becky:
Here, miss? Me?

(Sara runs to the door, opens it, and looks out and listens).

Sara:
No-one is anywhere about, your bedrooms are finished, perhaps you might stay a tiny while. I thought—perhaps—you might like a piece of cake.

(Sara opens a cupboard and gives her a thick slice of cake).

Becky:

Is that— (*looking longingly at Sara's rose-colored frock*). Is that there your best dress?

Sara:

It is one of my dancing-frocks. I like it, don't you?

Becky:

Once I seen a princess. I was standin' in the street with the crowd outside Coven' Garden, watchin' the swells go inter the opera. An' there was one everyone stared at most. They ses to each other, 'That's the princess.' She was a growed-up young lady, but she was pink all over—gowned an' cloak, an' flowers an' all. I called her to mind the minnit I see you, sittin' there on the table, miss. You looked like her.

Sara:

I"ve often thought that I should like to be a princess; I wonder what it feels like. I believe I will begin pretending I am one. Becky, weren't you listening to that story?

Becky:

Yes, miss, I knowed I hadn't orter, but it was that beautiful I—I couldn't help it.

Sara:

I like you to listen to it. If you tell stories, you like nothing so much as to tell them to people who want to listen. I don't know why it is. Would you like to hear the rest?

Becky:

Me hear it? Like as if I was a pupil, miss! All about the Prince—and the little white Mer-babies swimming about laughing—with stars in
their hair?

Sara:

You haven't time to hear it now, I'm afraid, but if you will tell me just what time you come to do my rooms, I will try to be here and tell you a bit of it every day until it is finished. It's a lovely long one—and I'm always putting new bits to it.

Becky:

Then, I wouldn't mind *how* heavy the coal boxes was—or *what* the cook done to me, if—if I might have that to think of.

Sara:

You may. I'll tell it *all* to you.

(When Becky goes downstairs, she is not the same Becky who staggered up, loaded down by the weight of the coal scuttle. She has an extra piece of cake in her pocket, and she has been fed and warmed).

(Alone) If I *was* a princess—a *real* princess, I could scatter largess to the populace. But even if I am only a pretend princess, I can invent little things to do for people. Things like this. She was just as happy as if it was largess. I'll pretend that to do things people like is scattering largess. I've scattered largess.

A LITTLE PRINCESS
BY FRANCES HODGSON BURNETT

(Sara Crewe has just found out that her father is dead and she no longer has funds to pay for her education at Miss Minchin's Academy. Miss Minchin rapidly makes it clear that Sara will now live in the attic with the other servants).

Miss Minchin:

Put down your doll, What do you mean by bringing her here?

Sara:

No, I will not put her down. She is all I have. My papa gave her to me.

(She makes Miss Minchin feel secretly uncomfortable. She does not speak with rudeness so much as with a cold steadiness with which Miss Minchin finds it difficult to cope).

Miss Minchin:

You will have no time for dolls in future, you will have to work and improve yourself and make yourself useful. Everything will be very different now, I suppose Miss Amelia has explained matters to you.

Sara:

Yes. My papa is dead. He left me no money. I am quite poor.

Miss Minchin:

You are a beggar. It appears that you have no relations and no home, and no one to take care of you. What are you staring at? Are you so stupid that you cannot understand? I tell you that you are quite alone in the world, and have no one to do anything for you, unless I choose to keep you here out of charity.

Sara:
I understand. I understand.

Miss Minchin:
That doll, that ridiculous doll, with all her nonsensical, extravagant things—I actually paid the bill for her!

Sara:
The Last Doll, The Last Doll!

Miss Minchin:
The Last Doll, indeed! And she is mine, not yours. Everything you own is mine.

Sara:
Please take her away from me, then, I do not want her.

Miss Minchin:
Don't put on grand airs, the time for that sort of thing is past.
You are not a princess any longer. Your carriage and your pony will be sent away—your maid will be dismissed. You will wear your oldest and plainest clothes—your extravagant ones are no longer suited to your station. You are like Becky—you must work for your living.

Sara:
Can I work? If can work it will not matter so much. What can I do?

Miss Minchin:
You can do anything you are told. You are a sharp child, and you pick up things readily. If you make yourself useful, I may let you stay here. You speak French well, and you can help with the younger children.

Sara:
May I? Oh, please let me! I know I can teach them. I like them, and they like me.

Miss Minchin:
Don't talk nonsense about people liking you. You will have to do more than teach the little ones. You will run errands and help in the kitchen as well as in the schoolroom. If you don't please me, you will be sent away. Remember that. Now go.

(She turns to leave the room).

Stop! Don't you intend to thank me?

Sara:
What for?

Miss Minchin:

For my kindness to you. For my kindness in giving you a home.

(Sara makes two or three steps toward her. Her thin little chest heaving up and down).

Sara:
You are not kind. You are *not* kind, and it is *not* a home.

(She turns and runs out of the room before Miss Minchin can stop her or do anything but stare after her with stony anger. She goes up the stairs slowly, and she holds Emily tightly against her side).

I wish you could talk, if you could speak—if only you could speak!

Miss Minchin:
You—you are not to go into that room any more.

Sara:
Not go in?

Miss Minchin:
That is not your room now.

Sara:
Where is my room?

Miss Minchin:
You are to sleep in the attic next to Becky.

A LITTLE PRINCESS
BY FRANCES HODGSON BURNETT

(Sarah is now living in the attic. Ermengarde is missing Sara's friendship and decides to pay her a visit).

Ermengarde:
Oh, Sara, is that you? Oh, how—how are you?

Sara:
I don't know. How are you?

Ermengarde:
I'm—I'm quite well Are you—are you very unhappy?

Sara:
What do you think? Do you think I am very unhappy What are you crying for, Ermengarde?

Ermengarde:
I'm not crying. Well, yes, I am. I'm miserable—and no one need interfere.

Sara:
Ermengarde! You will get into trouble.

Ermengarde:
I know I shall—if I'm found out. But I don't care—I don't care a bit. Oh, Sara, please tell me. What is the matter? Why don't you like me anymore, Sara?

Sara:
I do like you, I thought—you see, everything is different now. I thought you—were different.

Ermengarde:
Why, it was you who were different! You didn't want to talk to me. I didn't know what to do.

Sara:
Yes, I *am* different, though not in the way you think. Miss Minchin does not want me to talk to the girls. Most of them

don't want to talk to me. I thought—perhaps—you didn't. So, I tried to keep out of your way.

Ermengarde:
Oh, Sara, I couldn't bear it anymore, I dare say you could live without me, Sara; but I couldn't live without you. I was nearly dead. So tonight, when I was crying under the bedclothes, I thought all at once of creeping up here and just begging you to let us be friends again.

Sara:
You are nicer than I am. I was too proud to try and make friends. You see, now that trials have come, they have shown that I am *not* a nice child. I was afraid they would. Perhaps— that is what they were sent for.

Ermengarde:
I don't see any good in them.

Sara:
Neither do I—to speak the truth, I suppose there *might* be good in things, even if we don't see it. There *might* - be good in Miss Minchin.

Ermengarde:
Sara, do you think you can bear living here?

Sara:
If I pretend it's quite different, I can, or if I pretend it is a place in a story. Other people have lived in worse places. Think of the Count of Monte Cristo in the dungeons of the Chateau d'If. And think of the people in the Bastille!

Ermengarde:
The Bastille!

Sara:
Yes, that will be a good place to pretend about. I am a prisoner in the Bastille. I have been here for years and years—and years; and everybody has forgotten about me. Miss Minchin is the jailer—and Becky - Becky is the prisoner in the next cell. I shall pretend that and it will be a great comfort.

<u>Ermengarde:</u>
And will you tell me all about it? May I creep up here at night, whenever it is safe, and hear the things you have made up in the day? It will seem as if we were more 'best friends' than ever.

<u>Sara:</u>
Yes. Adversity tries people, and mine has tried you and proved how nice you are.

I CAPTURE THE CASTLE
BY DODIE SMITH

(Two sisters, Rose and Cassandra, live in a Castle. Rose is engaged to a young American man but does not genuinely love him. She is hoping his wealth may help to save the family home. Meanwhile, her younger sister, Cassandra, has developed feelings for him).

Cassandra:
I won't try to find out if Rose cares for him – what's the use? And I mustn't, I mustn't let her know about me.
(Rose enters)

Rose:
Topaz is actually dancing across the courtyard. She gets more bogus every day.

Cassandra:
Yet somehow, she's genuine too. How mixed people are. How mixed and. nice. Oh, honeysuckle!

Rose:
Messy stuff. Simon stopped the car to gather me some.

Cassandra:
Rose! You don't love him.

Rose:
No. Pity, isn't it?

Cassandra:
Why did you lie to me the night you engaged?

Rose:
I didn't. When he kissed me, it was – well, exciting. I thought that meant I was in love. You wouldn't understand. You're too young.

Cassandra:
I understand, all right. How long have you known?

Rose:
For ages. But it's got worse since I went to London – he's with me so much more there. Every minute we're together I can feel him *asking* for love. He somehow links it with everything – if it's a lovely day or we see anything beautiful. Oh, it's such a comfort to talk to you.

Cassandra:
Poor Rose. Would you like me to tell him for you?

Rose:
Tell him? Oh, I'm still going to marry him.

Cassandra:
You are not. You're not going to do anything so wicked.

Rose:
Why is it suddenly wicked? You helped me get him long before
you thought I was in love with him.

Cassandra:
I didn't understand. It was just fun – like something in a book. It wasn't real.

Rose:
Well, it's real enough now.

Cassandra:
You can't do it, Rose – not just for clothes and jewelry.

Rose:
You talk as if I'm doing it all for myself. Do you know what my last thought has been, night after night? At least they've had enough to eat at the castle today. And I've thought of you more than anyone – of all I'm going to do for you.

Cassandra:
Then you can stop thinking – because I won't take anything from you. And you can stop pretending to be noble. You're going to wreck his whole life. When he's the most wonderful person who ever lived…

Rose:
You're in love with him yourself. Oh, no! Darling, listen. I swear I'd give him up if he'd marry you instead. I'd be glad to because he'd still go on helping us. I don't want a lot of luxury – but I won't let us all go back to such hideous poverty. And we'd have to if I gave him up, because he'd never fall in love with you. He thinks of you as a little girl.

Cassandra:
What he thinks of me has got nothing to do with it. It's *him* I'm thinking of.

Rose:
Do you realise what would happen if I broke the engagement? He'd let Scoatney Hall to the Fox-Cottons and go back to America with Neil. How would you like that?

Cassandra:
You're not going to marry him without loving him.

Rose:
Don't you know he'd rather have me that way than not at all?

(A motor horn is heard)

There's the car back. We'll talk again. I'm supposed to be staying at Scoatney tonight, but I'll say I want to be with you. We'll try to help each other.

Cassandra:
If you come back here, I won't speak to you. And I'm not coming to Scoatney. I'm not going to watch you show your power over him.

<u>Rose</u>:
But you must come. What'll they think if you don't?

<u>Cassandra</u>:
Tell him I have a headache!

<u>Rose</u>:
If you knew how wretched I am…

<u>Cassandra</u>:
Go and make a list of your trousseau – that'll cheer you up. You grasping little cheat.

<u>Rose</u>:
You're failing me just when I need you most.

AUTHOR INDEX

Peter Pan by J.M. Barrie (1911)
The Wizard of Oz by L. Frank Baum(1900)

Alice in Wonderland by Lewis Carroll (1865)
The Secret Garden by Frances Hodgson Burnett (1911)
The Snow Queen by Hans Christian Anderson (1844) Puss in Boots by Perrault (1697)
Toad of Toad Hall by Kenneth Grahame (1929)
The House at Pooh Corner by A.A.Milne
Tom Sawyer by Mark Twain (1876)
Pinocchio by Carlo Collodi (1883)
Puss in Boots by Charles Perrault (1697)
Lord Arthur Savile's Crime by Oscar Wilde (1891)
The Importance of Being Earnest by Oscar Wilde (1895)
Winnie the Pooh by A. A. Milne (1926)
The Ugly Duckling by A.A. Milne (1941)
A Little Princess by Frances Hodgson Burnett (1905)

The Snow Queen by Hans Christian Andersen (1844) Little Women by Louisa May Alcott (1868)
Rebecca of Sunnybrook Farm by K D.Wiggin (1903)
Back to Methuselah by George Bernard Shaw (1921)
Pygmalion by George Bernard Shaw (1912)
The Secret Garden by Frances Hodgson Burnett (1911)
The Princess & The Players by Barbara Watts (1934)
Beauty & the Beast by G. S. Barbot de Villeneuve (1740)
Anne of Green Gables by L.M Montgomery (1908)
I Capture the Castle by Dodie Smith (1948)

ABOUT THE AUTHOR

Kim Gilbert trained as a professional actress at the Guildford School of Acting, studied for an LGSM with the Guildhall School of Music and Drama and took an English degree at the Open University. She has been acting, teaching and directing plays and musical productions for more than 35 years. She has experience in a wide range of theatre, TV and voiceover work. She has a First-class Honours degree in English and has taught English and Drama in many top schools in the country. Kim has examined for Lamda for a number of years and has also acted as an adjudicator. She has been running Dramatic Arts Studio for 13yrs, a private drama studio which specialises in developing excellence in all forms of performance and communication.

Other Books by the same author:

Shakespeare Scenes

Monologues for young adult female actors
Monologues for young female actors
Duologues for female actors
Monologues for young male actors
Duologues for male & female actors
Duologues for two male actors

Chekhov Scenes

Monologues & Duologues for women
Monologues for Male Actors

Scenes from Oscar Wilde

Monologues & Duologues for female actors
Monologues for Male actors
Duologues from Oscar Wilde

Monologues & Duologues from Charles Dickens

Scenes from George Bernard Shaw:
Monologues & Duologues

Classic Scenes

Classic Monologues for female actors
Classic Duologues for female actors
Classic Acting Monologues for Girls (8-14yrs)
Classic Acting Monologues for Boys (8-14yrs)
Acting Duologues for boys & girls aged 5-10
Acting Monologues for girls aged 5-10

Improve Your Voice
How to speak English with confidence

Available from Amazon Bookstore

Thank you for reading! If you enjoyed this book or found it useful, I would be grateful if you'd post a short review on Amazon. Your support really does make a difference and I read all the reviews personally so I can get your feedback and make this book even better. Thank you for your support

Printed in Great Britain
by Amazon